MW00966037

To the memory of my mom,
Margaret Anne O'Brien (1936–2005),
who impacted my heart with
optimism and vision
at a very young age.

Contents

Key #5: Express Your Uniqueness

Acknowledgements

This book would not have been a reality without the prayers and encouragement of friends and family members. Thank you for believing in me and in the fulfillment of my dreams.

I would like to acknowledge a few of those who helped make this book possible.

I am thankful for my children, Miriam, Abby, and Jeremy, for your love and patience with me throughout this creative process. You have been the reason I have kept writing.

For my first husband, Darwin Dewar, although he did not get to see this book in print before he died, his consistent love, faith, and godly example empowered me to live these truths and become who I am today.

My mother's optimism, joy, and faith during my childhood days modelled to me the power of not letting circumstances define who you are. I am forever grateful for the qualities she passed on to me.

To the many friends who have stood with me throughout the different seasons of my life, your patience, kindness, and ongoing support have strengthened and inspired me to keep moving forward.

To my husband, David, who came into my life at just the right time, thank you for loving me for who I am and for demonstrating what it means to cultivate heart-centred relationships. Your love, prayers, and constant encouragement fuel my every step with greater passion.

To all the people who have given me the honour of being a part of their transformation journey, this book would not have been possible without you taking the risk to engage your heart and embrace the processes of God with courage and commitment.

Introduction

Since 1989, I have been actively involved in working with people in the areas of spiritual direction, personal development, and transformation. I have had the privilege of working with people from all walks of life and diverse cultural backgrounds. No matter who they are or where they were born, all have the same basic needs and yearnings: to be loved, accepted, and free to live the lives they were created for.

In addition to cultural and spiritual mindsets, the biggest blocks I have seen holding people back originate in their inability to connect intimately at the heart level. The Greatest Commandment in the Bible tells us to love with our whole hearts, first God and then others. Our modern cultures have not trained us in the importance of living in a place of deep connection to the most central part of our being: our hearts. We approach relationships and our spiritual journey cerebrally and wonder why we feel empty.

The purpose of this book is to empower you to start living the real you, how God designed you. It focuses on understanding your true identity, embracing your uniqueness, and discovering the five keys to experiencing wholeness and freedom every day. Living true to yourself will require courage, compassion, and learning to celebrate. You must be willing to connect more deeply, with your own heart, with the heart of God, and with the hearts of those with whom you interact.

Wholeness and freedom are not only attained after we die. An extraordinary life of joy, peace, and freedom from fear is yours to access while living on the earth. Not only is it possible, but it is essential if you want to experience the richer, more fulfilling life you are wired for. Wholeness and freedom are yours to experience every day if you dare to engage your heart, courageously step out of your comfort zone, and trust the Holy Spirit to walk you through the process.

In their book, *Sacred Romance*, authors Brent Curtis and John Eldredge describe the Christian life as, above all else, "a love affair of the heart. It cannot be lived primarily as a set of principles or ethics. It cannot be managed with steps and programs. It cannot be lived exclusively as a moral code leading to righteousness."[1]

Portions of this book were first published under a different title: *Let the Real U Step Forward*.[2] After interacting more with the truths, I realized that readers need to more explicitly understand the topics of freedom and identity in Christ in order to more intentionally embrace the process of transformation and actively engage a life of wholeness and holiness every day. *Let the Real You Step Forward Now* is primarily a revision of the first book, and it aims to show not only the importance of your active choice in moving forward, but why you need to start stepping forward now, every day. It's not about passively waiting for God to position you, but rather about embracing the truth and choosing to walk in it moment by moment. This will mean choosing to let go of some things that threaten to keep you stuck in order to free you to move forward. In most cases, what you choose to let go of is more critical than what you grab hold of.

Whenever I read the book of James in the Bible, I'm struck by its message of relevance and wisdom in helping me navigate through uncertain times. One time while I was reading through the first chapter of James, I got excited to discover the choice of wording in the New Living Translation version:

> *Dear brothers and sisters, when troubles of any kind come your way, consider it an opportunity for great joy. For you know that when your faith is tested, your endurance has a chance to grow. So let it grow, for when your endurance is fully developed, you will be perfect and complete, needing nothing.*
>
> —James 1:2–4

Do you want to be strong in character? Do you want to be ready for anything that comes your way? Then get out of your own way, embrace a growth mindset, and give yourself permission to step forward to engage the opportunities God brings your way, even if you don't understand the full picture.

In the creation account in the book of Genesis, God said, *"Let there be light"* (Genesis 1:3), *"Let the waters beneath the sky flow together"* (Genesis 1:9), and *"Let the land sprout with vegetation"* (Genesis 1:11). On and on He spoke until the completion of all He wanted to create on the earth at that time. When He created the first man, Adam, He said, *"Let us make human beings in our image"* (Genesis 1:26). I believe that even when you were formed in your mother's womb, God declared over you, "Let (put your name here) be formed according to My perfect design!"

The word *let* includes a meaning that is pivotal for causing change to happen, for new things to emerge, for creativity to flow, and for hearts to be awakened. It implies an authority to bring something into everyday reality, that currently only exists in seed form as a desire in your heart.

It is my hope that as you continue through the following chapters, you will discover the importance of living the real you, of engaging your heart, embracing transformation, and finally experiencing the freedom Jesus died to bring you. I pray that you will be empowered to not settle for anything less than walking in the fullness of God.

Choosing a life of freedom and wholeness can bring up all kinds of emotions and resistance, depending on your perceptions. If you're like me, experiences in your past have coloured how you see life today, and this affects your responses to what happens to you. Depending on how you've responded to past experiences, you may see life through a specific lens based on decisions you've made along the way. If the lens is clear, you're apt to see what is really happening; however, it's more likely that you have distorted perceptions (as we all do) and barriers that prevent you from fully embracing opportunities in life. God wants to take you through a process to see and feel like He does, and to walk in wholeness, holiness, and complete joy no matter what you have experienced in the past!

This is the loving process God takes each of us through as part of restoring us and enabling us to live true to who we were designed to be and to reflect His nature more clearly. It will require courage, compassion, humility, and wholehearted loving. Are you ready to learn how to pursue wholeness and freedom? Are you ready to expand your capacity to experience a life of intimacy, adventure, and extraordinary joy? Great! Let us step forward together now!

Endnotes

1   Brent Curtis and John Eldredge, *The Sacred Romance: Drawing Closer to the Heart of God* (Nashville, TN: Thomas Nelson, 1997), 8.

2   Lisa Vanderkwaak, *Let the Real U Step Forward* (Bloomington, IN: Westbow Press, 2012).

For you died to this life, and your real life is hidden with Christ in God.

—Colossians 3:3

Key #1
ENGAGE THE HEART

Life is a journey of the heart that requires the mind, not the other way around.[3]

—John Eldredge

chapter one

Designed for Connection

The true heart of relationships is connection. Deep, meaningful relationships are built by developing authentic connections with one another that recognize, inspire and nurture our unique spirits.[4]

—Dr. Joseph Umidi

"That's it," I decided when I was fifteen years old, feeling hurt and rejected by my family members. "I don't need them. I can live without them."

The people who were supposed to protect and care for me were refusing to support me when I needed it most, so I decided to close off my heart, trust only myself, and prove that I could make it on my own. You may wonder how that worked out for me. Not very well. In fact, I discovered that the very things I tried to push away—love and relationships—were the very things I needed most. The walls I put up in my heart to protect myself from getting hurt didn't draw a distinction between receiving love and avoiding pain. It kept everything good out and everything bad in.

Perhaps you're like most people and can recall more instances in your past when you felt disconnected from someone rather than connected. If you got hurt too many times, you may have believed that it was safer to shut down part of your heart and not "feel" anymore. The discomfort of disconnection often leads people to seek out ways to numb the pain just to survive. If that's true for you I want to ask you a question. What is that costing you emotionally, relationally, and spiritually? What effect is it having on your life?

Brené Brown, a social worker and researcher, set out to understand more about the relationship between human connection and shame. Little did she know that after six years of collecting data, her findings would lead her to experience a spiritual awakening. Her discoveries led to breakthroughs not only in her field of study, but also in her own life when her cognitive approach to life was challenged. During one of her TED talks, called "The Power of Vulnerability,"[5] Brown confessed that her findings led her down a path on which she rediscovered who she really was. This forever changed the way she approached life, love, and work.

In addition to humans being hardwired neurobiologically to seek connection with others, her findings now suggest that it is within the context of such connection that life becomes more fulfilling. Her studies have shown that one of the key elements to being able to live wholeheartedly is engaging in heart-centred connection. She went on to conclude, "Connection is why we are here. It is what gives purpose and meaning to our lives."[6]

True connection happens when the heart is willing to be seen. In his book *Waking the Dead*, author John Eldredge said,

> To remain present to God, you must remain present to your heart. To hear His voice, you must listen with your heart. To love Him, you must love with all your heart. You cannot be the person God meant you to be, and you cannot live the life He meant you to live, unless you live from the heart.[7]

As you read that quote, you may have inwardly protested, "But isn't it dangerous to live from the heart?" Yes, it can be, if your heart is filled with unresolved brokenness and pain. However, it's just as dangerous to live solely from your head, logic, and limited understanding. When you embrace the processes of transformation and wholeness, your heart becomes awakened and experiences a series of shifts. As you learn to align your heart to God's, it actually becomes more destructive to *not* live from your heart. Author and pastor Erwin McManus said in his book *The Barbarian Way* that if God "has won your heart then to follow your heart will always lead you to follow the heart of God."[8]

Both psychology and science tell us that the emotional responses to life's experiences are stored deeply within a person's heart. This is confirmed in the writings of King Solomon in Proverbs: *"Guard your heart above all else, for it determines the course of your life"* (Proverbs 4:23).

Like me, you may have had messages written on your heart that became the truth by which you live your life. Even though your heart has interpreted these messages as truth, they are simply beliefs and conclusions you formed based on your perceptions. If perceptions go unchallenged and not clarified, they become your reality. What you believe in your heart to be true drives your actions and determines the course of your life.

The danger is when these beliefs are not actually true, when they hinder you from stepping forward and fully living the real you. As you learn to connect at the heart level, you will become more in tune with what's going on inside you and be able to identify beliefs that may be blocking you from experiencing a richer, more fulfilling life.

Meaningful connections take place at the heart level. In the ancient Hebrew mindset, the term *heart* meant something different than in our Western culture. In English translations of the Bible, the word heart is substituted with *mind, emotions*, or the *will*. The Hebrew concept of the heart, however, includes all three of these concepts and more. It is the centre of one's being, the soul of a person. Just as the physical heart is the vital organ that feeds life and affects all the others, so it is with your spiritual heart. It is the core of who you are, affecting every part of how you live.

The ancient book of Proverbs says that it is from within the heart that all the issues of life are stored and released. Everything that concerns you is contained in and affected by your heart. Some biblical scholars even suggest that the boundaries of your life are set by what you believe to be true in your heart. If you feel stuck in any area, take a look at what you believe to be true about it. This may reveal the keys to getting unstuck.

If your heart is pure and healthy, so will your relationships and attitudes toward life. This is illustrated in biblical passages which suggest that having a pure heart helps you to see, or know, God clearly. As you think and believe in your heart, so will you act. The heart is central to how you do life. When you give your heart to something or someone, you are giving your *all*—including the most sacred part of you.

God places greater importance on the inner character than the outward appearance, as is highlighted when Jesus said of the religious leaders, *"These people honor me with their lips, but their hearts are far from me"* (Matthew 15:8).

Jesus once told a story about an unforgiving servant to illustrate the importance of not just forgiving with words but with heartfelt sincerity. He said that it isn't enough to give mental assent; we need to learn to forgive someone from the heart (Matthew 18:35).

These and other passages reveal that God places high importance on speaking, believing, and living from the heart. The problem comes when we don't know how to face, or are afraid of facing, the pain of unresolved issues hidden deep within. Fear of being seen and being rejected can hinder you from living the real you. Fear of engaging the heart can keep you from becoming whole and enjoying true freedom.

As you step forward in this adventure of learning to engage your heart and cultivate intimacy, you will need to keep in mind the following four principles.

1. Your perception affects connection. How you see yourself is often an indication of what you believe God thinks of you. If you are unable to connect with your own heart, you will be unable to connect with others. What you believe to be true about yourself will be reflected in your actions and relationships. Your perceptions create your reality. If left unchallenged, your distorted perceptions lead to deception.

2. You are created for intimacy. Extreme independence, self-sufficiency and shame are barriers to experiencing meaningful connections with others. You are wired for love and intimacy. God is love and you are created to walk in His likeness and operate in the same character and nature that Jesus demonstrated on the earth. Before I could receive love, though, I had to become aware of my need for love. Then, the more I opened my heart to receive God's love, the more His love flowed through me to others. When you have unresolved pain, it's easy to convince yourself that you don't need anyone. This is a lie we believe, a false protection that leads to further isolation and religious deception. You were created for intimacy, for wholehearted relationships.

> **If you are unable to connect with your own heart, you will be unable to connect with others.**

The late Jack Frost, in his book *Experiencing the Father's Embrace*, wrote that "God wants us to have fellowship with Him but a true relationship with [Him] will not come at the expense of intimacy with our spouses and families and friends."[9] He went on to explain that if you spend the majority of your time serving the needs of other people or keeping yourself locked away in a prayer closet, spending very little time intimately connecting with your spouse, then your life is unhealthy and out of order. Choosing to embrace intimacy, first with God, is a prerequisite to living in wholeness and holiness. However, the process of becoming whole is only fully realized as you regularly engage in authentic human interactions. You will discover that the place where you've gotten hurt is usually the same place God uses to heal you.

3. You alone are responsible for the ongoing condition of your heart. When we experience conflict or difficulty in relationships, our first reaction is often to blame the other person. This defence mechanism started in the Garden of Eden when Adam blamed Eve and God, saying, *"[God,] it was the woman you gave me"* (Genesis 3:12).

In order to learn how to love deeply and connect intimately with others, you need to be willing to take responsibility for the emotional and spiritual condition of your heart. Only you are able to feel where your heart may be experiencing resistance and is unable to receive and give love. You need to own your mistakes and seek help to resolve the issues that are keeping you stuck. Instead of trying to hide behind perfectionism, performance, or even self-pity, be willing to let yourself be open to lasting transformation. Choose truth over lies and walk in freedom and wholeness.

4. Fulfillment flows from connection. Not only are you hardwired neurobiologically for connection with others, but you are also wired spiritually for connection with God. You are designed to be in relationship with your Creator. The Ultimate Designer put His stamp on you and called you by name.

In the book of Genesis, the creation story includes a description of how God created Man. It says that God breathed into Man and made them into living beings. He created them in the image of God, both male and female.

The first couple, Adam and Eve, enjoyed perfect unity with God and with each other, communicating spirit to spirit. They lacked nothing because everything they needed flowed from their spiritual connection with their source of life and love. They were complete. This was God's original plan for your spirit, to be joined to His Spirit as your primary means of communication, love, joy, and fulfillment.

From the place of being spiritually connected to God, Adam and Eve received wisdom and truth from God's Spirit to their hearts. Their spirit then informed their bodies and souls what to do.

But when the couple chose to ignore their spirits and follow another voice, it resulted in spiritual and relational disconnection. In doing so, they gave up the intimacy, power, and authority that flowed from being connected spiritually to God, and as a result they became ruled by logic. The spirit of man then disconnected from its source of life and love. At that moment, they began to experience things they had never experienced before, and they perceived life differently. Fear, shame, insecurity, judgment, and blame entered their hearts. They suddenly saw their vulnerability as shameful and something to be hidden, whereas before it had been part of their beauty, something they had embraced and shared as part of their humanity.

From that one decision, all human beings were infected with the scars of disconnection and are forever unable to re-establish a relationship with God by human effort alone. Who you are at the core is spiritual, and therefore true wholeness and freedom begins when your soul becomes aware of your deep need for connection with Jesus and your spirit becomes awakened to the reality of who He really is and how much He loves you.

It was out of His love and a desire to be in relationship with his children that God provided a means to restore us to that place of belonging. He destroyed the barriers between us and invited us to exchange our broken and hardened hearts, which feared intimacy, for one that is tender and able to know love and be filled with desire to engage fully. In Jeremiah 24:7, we get a glimpse of this new heart: *"I will give them hearts that recognize me as the Lord. They will be my people, and I will be their God, for they will return to me wholeheartedly."*

When you accept God's invitation to reconnect spiritually with Him, He offers you a new heart that's aligned to the heart of God. Ezekiel 36:26–27 describes this great exchange:

> *And I will give you a new heart, and I will put a new spirit in you. I will take out your stony, stubborn heart and give you a tender, responsive heart. And I will put my Spirit in you so that you will follow my decrees and be careful to obey my regulations.*

While writing this chapter, my laptop kept freezing and shutting down because its memory was overloaded and couldn't handle any more new information. That's similar to what happens to us emotionally when we carry around unresolved issues in our hearts. The pain and negative emotions cloud our ability to process new information and often cause us to "check out" of life.

Think of this new heart as an upgraded operating system that's wired to the culture of heaven and to God's Spirit. Accepting this new heart and embracing God's love awakens your spiritual senses and expands your capacity to live and love more fully. From this place of connection, a whole new world of possibilities opens up to you and you can begin to approach life differently. You gain increased confidence in who you are and the courage to embrace your uniqueness and let the real you step forward.

Stepping Forward

- In what relationships do you find yourself blocked from receiving or giving love?
- Set aside time today to open your heart and invite God to reveal His love to you.
- What one step can you take today to begin to engage your heart to cultivate intimacy?
- Journal your discoveries.

Endnotes

3   John Eldredge, *Journey of Desire: Searching for the Life We've Only Dreamed Of* (Nashville, TN: Thomas Nelson, 2000), 202.

4   Dr. Joseph Umidi, "The Power of Transformational Conversations," *Compass MAP™ Coachcast*. December 19, 2009.

5   Brené Brown, "The Power of Vulnerability," *TED*. June 2010 (https://www.ted.com/talks/brene_brown_on_vulnerability).

6   Ibid.

7   John Eldredge, *Waking the Dead: The Glory of a Heart Fully Alive* (Nashville, TN: Thomas Nelson, 2006), 49.

8   Erwin McManus, *The Barbarian Way: Unleash the Untamed Faith Within You* (Nashville, TN: Thomas Nelson, 2005), 14.

9   Jack Frost, *Experiencing the Father's Embrace* (Shippensburg, PA: Destiny Image, 2002), 45.

chapter two

Your Ultimate Connection

The heart is the connecting point, the meeting place between any two persons. The kind of deep soul intimacy we crave with God and with others can be experienced only from the heart.[10]

—John Eldredge

The book of John says that eternal life means knowing God in such a way that you experience Him at a heart level (John 17:3). It is not an experience reserved for after you die but rather one that involves spiritually relating to God while you're here on the earth. The word *know* in this passage means to be intimately connected with someone. It's an experiential knowing. Knowing God in this way means something more than giving mental assent to the fact that He's real; it involves relating to God with a heart that's fully engaged. The eternal life you are invited to enjoy is vibrant, joy-filled, and extremely fulfilling. This extravagant life begins when you become born again and continues as you choose daily to engage your heart in getting to know God.

One of my favourite passages is found in John 15:5. The writer sets things straight as to the type of relationship that is possible, saying that as you stay connected to God your life will become productive and fulfilling. However, when you are disconnected from Him you can do nothing. If a branch is lying beside a tree, it will eventually shrivel up and die if it's not attached to the trunk. When securely connected, the branch can easily draw nourishment, strength, and everything it needs from the tree's root system and produce healthy fruit.

This is the kind of relationship God designed you to have. By connecting spiritually to His Spirit, you have access to everything you need to thrive in life and relationships. He invites you into this relationship and will coach you every step of the way towards experiencing wholeness.

The first step is being willing. As you choose to open your heart, you may see things that you don't like or that are painful. You may be tempted to simply run in the other direction. Don't run! This is the time to tap into God as your source of comfort and draw from Him the courage to face your fears and run *towards* Him. It is God's desire that you be whole and fully alive in spirit, soul, and body. As you seek to know Him intimately and allow Him into those areas of your heart that may be locked up, frozen, or wounded, you will begin to experience freedom and joy like you never imagined. Yes, it may involve some uncomfortable moments, but the rewards will far outweigh the cost. Eternal life is a gift you can enjoy every day, experiencing the full measure of God's heart for you, if you want it.

Knowing God

But those who wish to boast should boast in this alone: that they truly know me and understand that I am the Lord who demonstrates unfailing love and who brings justice and righteousness to the earth, and that I delight in these things.
—Jeremiah 9:24

Do you know someone who likes to brag about knowing certain famous or important people and is always name-dropping? It can be annoying, can't it? When someone does that, it's usually a sign of insecurity, as they believe others will value them more because of who they know. Well, God said that it's actually okay for us to boast about understanding and knowing Him!

In our culture, we often use the word *know* very casually, although in most instances it would be more accurate to say that we are acquainted with others. When scriptures invite us to know God, however, it means something far deeper than merely getting acquainted.

Kevin Dedmon, pastor and author, describes how the ancient Hebrew word *yada*, which is translated in the English as "knowing," is used throughout scripture. He argues that the word, depending on its use, could mean "to know" in one of five distinct dimensions.[11] To understand what it means to connect with God more intimately and to embrace the transformation process, it would be helpful to look more closely at what these five dimensions are and how we can experience them.

Note that the equivalent Greek word, used in the New Testament, is *ginoski*, and it is similarly interpreted.

1. Knowing someone in detail. This refers to the act of studying or investigating a person like a detective until you know them thoroughly. Paul prays in

Ephesians 1:17 for the believers to have "spiritual wisdom and insight so that you might grow in your knowledge of God." The Greek word used for knowledge here is *epignosis* and expresses the process of actively pursuing God. This passage also implies that there is still more of God to know, and sometimes we are required to have a supernatural understanding of details in order to know Him more.

2. Knowing someone technically. This dimension refers not only to having a knowledge that God exists, but also to know *how* He works. It means knowing His ways, as Moses did (Exodus 33:13), and how to experience His presence in our lives. This involves becoming familiar with God's character and His way of acting. Once you know God in this manner, you will be able to identify the subtleties of deception and messages that declare a way that seems good and right but is not God's way! This type of knowing Him has grown increasingly necessary in this time of history.

3. Knowing someone by personal experience. Lasting transformation happens when we encounter God at a heart level, when we experience Him in such a way that our knowing moves from head knowledge to heart knowledge. I once heard John Arnott, the founding pastor of the Toronto Airport Church, reflect on his fifty years as a Christian and say, "My only regret is that it took me far too long to discover the foundational importance of the love of God. I am referring to the eighteen-inch journey, where truth goes from the head to the heart, where truth is *caught* rather than merely *taught*." This type of knowing cements a truth in your heart, making it immovable. This is the meaning of the word used in Philippians 3:10: *"I want to know Christ and experience the mighty power that raised him from the dead. I want to suffer with him, sharing in his death…"*

Even though I have made a commitment to be a lifelong learner, and I encourage everyone to do the same, I realize that education (knowledge) by itself is ineffective if it doesn't penetrate the heart. This was confirmed to me by a quote I read recently, attributed to Francis de Sales, a bishop in Geneva in the 1600s: "Your education has been a failure no matter how much it has done for your mind, if it has failed to open your heart."

Jesus rebuked the religious leaders of His day for believing that simply gaining knowledge of God was the way to know Him. In John 5:39, Jesus said, *"You search the Scriptures because you think they give you eternal life. But the Scriptures point to me!"* Those religious leaders valued knowledge about God above knowing Him through relationship.

In order to reflect God's nature accurately in your life, you will require a desire to go beyond simply knowing God in your mind to knowing Him intimately and experientially. You may learn the characteristics of God's nature from other people, or from reading scriptures, such as His role as a comforter. But only when you experience Him comforting you can you truly say with confidence, "God is my Comforter."

Once you know God by experience, no one can steal that truth from you; it has been imprinted on your heart. This is part of what it means to know the truth in such a way that it makes you free.

To know God in this way, you must give Him the opportunity to make Himself known. With every opportunity you take to cooperate with the work of the Holy Spirit in your life, God will reveal to you another aspect of His nature in a profound way. These God moments, or encounters, are important when it comes to establishing certain foundations in your life, including trust, identity, and truth.

As you come to know God more, you will become transformed into His likeness and be free to live as He designed you to be.

I can tell countless stories from my own life that testify to this process. One occurred when I had moved to Vancouver to complete a graduate degree at the University of British Columbia. The program I enrolled in was very intense and students were urged to have the financial backing to carry them through the two years without getting an outside job.

I had just finished a four-year undergraduate degree where I had worked two to three jobs at the same time throughout my full-time studies. Being told that for two years I wouldn't have the time for a part-time job posed a faith challenge to me. I believed the Scriptures when they said that God was my provider, but now I had an opportunity to know this part of His nature in a personal and experiential way. I could have put off my studies until I had saved enough money, but I sensed God inviting me to know Him in this way, so I trusted Him and took the risk. I applied for the program and was accepted.

I chose to thank God for His provision many times throughout those two years, even before I saw it in my hand. As I committed to knowing God as my provider, I began to receive money in various ways, and it was always enough to pay for rent, school fees, and food.

One month, I didn't have enough money to buy food for the coming two weeks. I prayed, asking God to provide, and then I thanked Him. Shortly after I ended my prayer, someone knocked on my door. It was a friend of mine, Larry, who had been driving home when a thought popped into his mind to buy a few extra groceries and bring them to me. So he followed the prompting of the Spirit and was used by God without even knowing my need.

On several other occasions, money came in the mail from people I didn't even know. During this season of learning, my dad showed up again in my life and wanted to pay for some of my expenses.

As I reached out to God for solutions to my problem, He faithfully came through. In the process of learning to trust Him in this way, He also began to invite me to lay down the unhealthy structures of pride and independence that were operating in my life as a result of my limiting beliefs. This was one of the keys that opened the door for further restoration in my relationship with my dad.

As I came to experience who God really was, I felt freer to trust Him to provide for me—and as I came to accept the truth of who He was, I chose to trust Him to protect my heart when I took the risk to trust others.

When God reveals an aspect of His character and nature to you in an experiential way, that truth becomes embedded in your heart. No one can tell you any differently. In the process, your identity becomes rooted and grounded in His love, and your heart more intimately connected to His.

4. Knowing someone through a face-to-face encounter. At first, this may seem to be the same as the previous dimension, but it isn't. This refers to an up close and personal relationship. It involves a degree of intimacy that allows you to look at someone's face, into their eyes and heart, so that you can hear the slightest whisper and the tender words of love. You can feel their embrace.

When it comes to knowing God in this way, it's the difference between religious performance and personal relationship. It means coming close to God with confidence that He loves you and desires to be with you. It means detecting the immediacy of His presence and openness of His heart. It means experiencing waves of joy and healing sweep over your soul as you embrace His love and truth more fully.

Have you ever felt suddenly overwhelmed by God's tangible presence while worshipping Him? Perhaps you saw a vision or heard His voice speak clearly and it made you come undone. In moments like this, when you have face-to-face encounters with God, your heart will melt and you will long to know Him even more. A passage in James 4:8 promises that if you pursue closeness with God, He will come closer to you: *"Come close to God, and God will come close to you."*

5. Knowing someone through sexual intimacy. It is important to note here that when it comes to knowing God in this way, we're not referring to the physical act of sex; rather, we're referring to the spiritual and emotional effects of knowing Him so intimately that you feel one with Him. Dedmon says that this type of knowing cannot be fully experienced until you have thoroughly experienced the first four dimensions.

The aim of *yada* is intimacy, and the fruit of such intimacy can be seen in how you relate to people. There's a depth of satisfaction that emerges in knowing that you are thoroughly loved by God.

1 John 3:9 says that God's seed is in us as a reminder of His commitment of love and to produce a life of fruitfulness. This fruitfulness is born out of an intimate relationship with God. Intimacy results as you come to know God in deeper ways and as you encounter Him up close and personal. As His love fills your heart, it naturally spills over into how you interact with others.

Several passages in the New Testament speak of Christ's relationship with the church being like that of a husband and wife. Indeed, the highest form of knowing another person intimately on the earth is the love between a man and a woman as they unite in marriage to become one. When you get to know your spouse intimately, you enter a place of extreme vulnerability and transparency. The real issues of the heart surface and can no longer be denied. You cannot hide.

As great as this intimate connection is between a husband and wife, those feelings of closeness, belonging, and satisfaction are only a foretaste of the profound intimacy that Jesus and His Bride will enjoy in eternity. The emotional and spiritual connectedness that occurs when a married couple engages in the physical act of making love serves as a reminder of the depth of spiritual intimacy God invites you to experience with Him.

Author Paula Rinehart discusses the parallels between sex and prayer in her book *Strong Women, Soft Hearts*. She acknowledges that we rarely hear those two words in the same sentence, yet they both contain the "elements of passion and surrender, the laying bare of the soul" before the Lord or your spouse, "with whom you have an exclusive relationship, unlike any other."[12]

This concept of knowing God may be hard to grasp for us in the western world, because our education has been so influenced by the Greek way of thinking. The Hebrew word *yada* has so many dimensions. Unlike the Greek mindset, the Hebrew understanding of truth didn't develop through a mental exercise but rather was experienced in body, soul, and spirit. Perhaps this is why Jesus presented Himself as the Truth, so that the religious leaders and His followers could grasp the personal and intimate dimensions of knowing God.

Rinehart believes that God created sexual intimacy as "a kind of physical patterning, an acting out of a spiritual mystery that hints of the utter pleasure we will know one day in the presence of the Lord."[13]

I personally believe that this isn't just reserved for the afterlife. I believe that it's possible to start knowing God in this dimension in the here and now, if you are willing to be vulnerable and transparent with Him in the deepest places of your heart. This dimension of knowing leads to a spiritual oneness that surpasses all other forms of intimacy known to mankind. It will penetrate the depths of your soul like nothing else. This is the path that leads to wholeness and freedom.

Benefits of Connection

Several years ago, I had the privilege of travelling to Africa to work with Home of Hope, a ministry based out of Red Deer, Alberta. One morning while we were ministering in Rwanda, and getting ready for the day, one of the young ladies on the team turned on her hair dryer in the bathroom. No sooner had she started drying her hair than the dryer suddenly made a sound like a small explosion and stopped working. Her hair dryer had blown up because it wasn't connected to the right power converter for the outlets in Africa. If she had connected her hair dryer to the right converter, she would have had access to all the power she needed.

That's what it's like when we choose to connect with God as our source of life. The Holy Spirit is like a power converter allowing the resources of heaven to flow in and through our human forms. If we try to bypass God's ways, it doesn't work.

Pursuing the heart of God will lead you to discover who you really are and what your divine purpose is. In addition, you will discover that you have the power to embrace life more fully through this connection, to love extravagantly and do even greater works than Jesus did. This is the life of fullness you were designed to live, and it starts with learning to engage your heart.

How to Connect

No amount of human effort can successfully restore you into relationship with Father God. You have been made in the image of God, and that includes being relational. But God isn't only relational; He is love personified. Out of His love for creation, He put a plan into action and provided a means for us to be intimately connected once again. This plan involved sending Jesus, His only Son, to the earth as a man to show us what it looks like to be intimately connected to Father God while living on the earth. This doesn't make sense to our natural minds, so if you're struggling to understand it, you're not alone. Ask God to give you supernatural insight and to reveal the truth of who Jesus was and what exactly His death and resurrection accomplished.

You see, if you're not spiritually connected to God through Jesus, you are connected to the world's way of doing life, which leads to temporary satisfaction and fleeting fulfillment. In order for you to connect to a holy God, you need someone to remove the barriers that stand between you and Him. The only person qualified to do that was Jesus, because He became a human yet didn't come under the world's way of living. He wasn't contaminated by sin. He was whole. Throughout His life, he stayed connected to Father God as His source of life and demonstrated holiness.

It was our choices that got us off track, and it will be our choices that get us back on track. Disconnection happens when we choose to live our lives selfishly, the way we want to, based on our own understanding.

To be restored spiritually, we need to admit our need for forgiveness and reconciliation. Forgiveness could only be accomplished when all the requirements of the Law were fulfilled. Jesus's death fulfilled all the requirements, and His blood was shed to remove all the barriers that stood in the way of us knowing God. That's what Jesus meant when He said, just before He died, *"It is finished!"* (John 19:30) He had completed the work He had been sent to the earth to do. All the requirements of the Law had been fulfilled through this one act.

> **It was our choices that got us off track, and it will be our choices that get us back on track.**

Now, you and I have the means to truly experience wholeness. By His resurrection, He demonstrated His power to overcome sin and continue to live in freedom. This same power is available to you today through *connection* with Jesus.

Exactly what was accomplished on the cross is described in Colossians 2:13–15:

> *You were dead because of your sins and because your sinful nature was not yet cut away. Then God made you alive with Christ, for he forgave all our sins. He canceled the record of the charges against us and took it away by nailing it to the cross. In this way, he disarmed the spiritual rulers and authorities. He shamed them publicly by his victory over them on the cross.*

By responding to the invitation to trust Him and accept the gift He's offering, you open your heart to become fully awakened to love, completely healed and transformed, and empowered to live in wholeness and holiness. Jesus did His part by removing the barriers that stood between you and God. His extravagant love made it possible for you to step forward with confidence and engage in intimate relationship with Father God.

By cooperating with the work of the Holy Spirit, you can continue the process of becoming all you were created to be. You will learn more about this process and exactly what your part involves in a later chapter, but for now it is essential to know that God's desire is that you experience Him fully and live in complete wholeness and freedom. Jesus demonstrated exactly how we can do this, by accessing the resources of heaven available to us to live a fulfilling, productive life.

Author John Eldredge reminds us in his book *Journey of Desire*, "We are made in the image of God, we carry within us the desire for our true life of intimacy and adventure."[14] Do you want to experience such a life? It starts by accepting Jesus's invitation to spiritually connect in relationship with Father God, by opening the door of your heart to receive His love, and by choosing to trust Him with your life.

Stepping Forward

- If you desire to start living this life of freedom and intimacy, accept God's invitation by responding like this:

  God, I realize that I have been spiritually disconnected from You and living life on my own terms. I accept that what Jesus did on the cross for me was enough to pay for my sins. I receive Your forgiveness and invite You into my heart to breathe new life into me. I welcome the work of Your Spirit to begin transforming me so that I may become who You created me to be and glorify You with the rest of my life. Thank You, Lord. Amen.

- Journal your discoveries.

Endnotes

10   John Eldredge, *Waking the Dead*, 48.

11   Kevin Dedmon, "Yada Yada Yada," *Kevin Dedmon*. September 16, 2014 (https://www.kevindedmon.com/blog/2014/9/16/yada-yada-yada).

12 Paula Rinehart, *Strong Women, Soft Hearts* (Nashville, TN: W Publishing Group, 2005), 139.

13 Ibid., 140.

14 John Eldredge, *Journey of Desire*, 166.

chapter three

Living from Your Heart

Guard your heart above all else, for it determines the course of your life.
—Proverbs 4:23

In the opening verse of Natalie Grant's song "In Better Hands," she sings, "You can't be free if you don't reach for help. It's hard to love when you don't love yourself." This is a spiritual concept, and it highlights the importance of attending to matters of your own heart. You can't properly love others if you don't love yourself. And you can't love yourself without knowing who you really are.

Jesus summarized the law of life this way: *"Love your neighbor as yourself"* (Matthew 19:19, 22:39). This passage isn't talking about some narcissistic way of living where you expect others to adjust to you. It refers to a healthy awareness of the greatness that lives inside you and the value you possess because you belong to God.

You are a masterpiece created by the greatest artist of all time! As you learn to reconnect with your own heart, you will get in touch with the way God wired you, the way He intended for you to function and the purpose you are meant to fulfill. By loving yourself, you are accepting who you are at the core and recognizing that your value and worth are unchangeable, no matter what has happened in your life. It is realize that you don't need to compete to be better than anyone or show anyone up. You don't need to prove your worth. You simply need to embrace who you are meant to be, with your strengths, gifts, and unique personality.

During my teenage years, my heart was charged with fear and bitterness. My environment was filled with constant chaos, destruction, and confusion. By the time I was fifteen, I had rejected certain aspects of myself that I judged to be shameful and unacceptable. However, in the process I also rejected parts of who I was. I had decided that I was going to be different. As a result, I determined to eliminate everything in my life that resembled my family and background. Because this response was born out of pain and bitterness, it eventually led me to shutting down parts of my heart and deny who I was at the core of my being. I disconnected myself from my heart and emotions and convinced myself that I could do better.

My pursuit to be someone else resulted in me becoming a perfectionist, an exercise addict, and eventually anorexic. I lost touch with myself, who I really was, and I approached life cold and guarded. I became very bitter and angry, refusing to trust anyone.

During this same time, my parents got divorced. Their marriage had been in trouble for many years and this tension spilled over into my life. Although appearing confident and together on the outside, inside I was plagued by fears and traumatized by confusing events.

Upon hearing news of the divorce from my mom, I felt a sense of hope. I thought to myself, *Yes, I'm finally free.* Yet my heart almost immediately cried with deep sadness, longing for love. As I battled about what to listen to, my head or my heart, I heard an audible voice say, "Read the Bible." This was a strange thought, because even though I had been brought up in a religious community we had never owned a Bible, nor had I ever been encouraged to read one.

After what seemed like hours of my head arguing with my heart, I finally decided to pay attention and follow my heart. In the midst of wondering where I could get my hands on a Bible, a thought came to me: I should write to trusted uncle and ask him to send one. A few weeks later, I received a parcel containing a full-sized Bible published by the Gideons.

I loved reading books, and as with any other book I started reading from the beginning. After reading the creation story, I found myself feeling bogged down by the genealogies and quickly skipped to the New Testament. It was there that I read about Jesus, and for the first time I became aware of my need for emotional healing and spiritual connection. Prior to that day, I'd thought I was a Christian. I had believed there was a God and heard about Jesus, but only after this encounter did I realize that I didn't know Him personally; I only knew about Him.

Throughout my childhood, I had done well in school, had been liked by others and always tried to do the right thing. However, when it came to matters of the heart I was filled with toxic emotions. I had judged my dad for being an alcoholic and for physically and emotionally abusing my mom. I'd decided that I couldn't trust him, so I had distanced myself in my heart and didn't want anything to do with him.

But on the day I learned about my parents' divorce, I became confused by the jarring awareness of what my heart really needed. Suddenly, I felt overwhelmed by a deep longing for a father's love. I tried to push the feelings away, but they only became stronger.

That day, as I read about Jesus, I became intrigued by the love He demonstrated and the words He spoke. I remember reading for hours past midnight about this amazing love and how it transformed lives. My heart filled with a desire to be like Him.

As I continued to read, it felt like God Himself came into my room, sat on my bed, and engaged me in heartfelt conversation. It was as if I was looking into a mirror, seeing the true condition of my heart and my desperate need for intimacy and love. All that I had tried to hide was suddenly exposed.

That initial spiritual encounter made me aware of three specific realities.

First, I became aware that I was disconnected from God and that my heart was filled with all the negative emotions I had judged my dad as having. In God's eyes, I was no different than the worst criminal.

Second, I realized that I needed God's forgiveness and emotional healing. Only His unconditional love could meet the cries of my heart for safety, security, and a father's love.

Third, I had a supernatural knowledge that I needed to forgive my dad. I became aware that I would never be free or have peace if I let the unforgiveness and pain stay in my heart.

That spiritual awakening started me on a journey of discovering who God really was and who He had made me to be. The more I opened my heart to know God, the more I began to discover the real me. As I pursued the life He had for me, I came to realize that I had shut my heart down in fear and believed lies. At the same time, the Holy Spirit showed me the truth and invited me to accept it. Accepting these truths empowered me to trust him step by step and ignited a desire in me to love and relate to others differently. My heart became freer to receive and give love. Whereas before I would have hidden and closed off my heart in fear of getting hurt, I was learning how to walk through my feelings of vulnerability and learning how to trust. For the first time, I began to feel alive on the inside and started to love myself.

The realization of God's love for me sank deeper into my heart and activated waves of healing, displacing the lies and destructive patterns of anorexia that I had been caught in. The more I let go of bitterness, pain and unforgiveness, the more I experienced healing and freedom, which in turn changed my relationships. My perspective on life shifted dramatically and I began to look at others with compassion and grace.

God's desire is for you to know who you are and learn to love yourself and value the unique person He made you to be. Your perception of yourself may be blurred by painful experiences or the limiting beliefs you have adopted. If you are willing to connect with God, tune in to your own heart, and ask God to show you who you really are, you can experience the power of His love flowing through you, teaching you how to love yourself. You can experience tremendous joy, peace, and fulfillment. It just requires the willingness to reconnect with your heart and be open to new possibilities, spiritually and relationally.

You cannot truly know another person unless you know yourself. Similarly, you cannot truly love another unless you love yourself. The degree to which you are able to connect with your own heart is the degree to which you will be able to connect deeply with another person. Remember, you were created for connection. It is in your DNA!

Common Barriers to Loving Who You Are

In his book *Deadly Emotions*, Dr. Don Colbert shows the connection between illness and a person's emotional condition. He describes differences in how the brain and the heart operate. He says that all toxic, damaging emotions are primarily stored in the heart. The problem comes when you don't listen to your heart and rely instead on your logic or understanding.

The brain is protective and territorial, and as such it is wired to pursue success and maintain equilibrium, whereas the heart is programmed to seek connection. When discussing the writings of Paul Pearsall, a neuropsychologist renowned for his research on the relationship between the brain, heart, and immune system,[15] Dr. Colbert explains that the brain can be compared to a type A personality whereas the heart functions more like a type B personality.

> The brain is always in a hurry and uncomfortable with just being somewhere. Type A behaviour—which is being critical, judgmental, harsh, cynical, blaming, controlling and unforgiving—is the behavior dramatically linked to disease. The Type B "heart" behavior, in contrast, is gentle, relaxed, and searching for long-lasting relationships and intimacy.[16]

While the brain seeks to have a blast, the heart seeks to have a bond. Dr. Colbert goes on to write,

When the brain remains in the driver's seat, the heart—the soul, the seat of the emotions—can be abused, wounded, exploited, and end up filled with hurt and pain. A heart that is filled with pain is a heart that is stressed, and often depressed.[17]

Even though the heart is the most powerful muscle in the human body, it can be severely strained by the pressures of the brain. Whenever we dismiss what our heart is trying to communicate to us and listen only to our mind, we suffer the dangerous consequences of what Paul Pearsall called "neglected heart syndrome."[18] This in turn can lead to negative patterns of abuse, deprivation, and exploitation of the most sensitive part of who you are. Colbert concluded that tuning into your own heart allows you to experience the child within you, which is the most sensitive part of your being, and which has the ability to awaken you to the joy of living.

It is clear that even medical science sees the health benefits of having an uncluttered and emotionally pure heart. As you seek to know yourself and pay attention to the movements within your heart, you may discover that you are stuck and unable to truly connect. This is very common and is often the point at which people give up.

If you truly want to know who you are and your unique purpose, it is essential that you pursue fullness of God, which leads to wholeness and freedom. Common barriers that threaten to keep you stuck include fear, shame, self-rejection, and limiting beliefs or distorted perceptions. Archibald D. Hart, in *The Bible for Hope: Caring for People God's Way*, writes, "When people conquer self-rejection, they open the door to be more accepting of both themselves and others."[19]

In a later chapter, you will learn the tools you need to overcome these blocks. Right now, it's important to determine how badly you want to be free to live the real you.

Practically speaking, how can you know the condition of your own heart? Most people would suggest that you start by asking yourself, "How do I feel today?" Dr. Colbert, however, says that to become aware of your own emotional state, you must instead ask yourself, "How do I make others feel?" The answer requires being honest with yourself as to whether you're devaluing the sensitivities in your own heart, as well as those of anyone who comes across your path. What you say and how you react reveal what's in your heart. As Luke 6:45 says, *"A good person produces good things from the treasury of a good heart, and an evil person produces evil things from the treasury of an evil heart. What you say flows from what is in your heart."*

Colbert goes on to say that it's especially important for you to own up to feelings of guilt or shame in your own heart, for they are "a vital key to unlocking health and wholeness."[20]

Proverbs 14:10 suggests that you are more aware of your own heart's condition than you realize. It says, *"Each heart knows its own bitterness, and no one else can fully share its joy."*

All the pain, hurt, disappointments, and shattered dreams of your life are stored deep within the recesses of your heart. Your mind and heart are often at odds with one another. Your beliefs about yourself, God, love, and life were formed over time and have emotions attached to them. To know yourself, you will need to learn how to access the emotional responses hidden within your soul. It is therefore essential that you learn to recognize the language of your own heart, to know what your heart is trying to say. Dr. Colbert summarized it this way: "To understand the depth of our own wounds, we each must learn the language of our own heart."[21]

> **What you say and how you react reveal what's in your heart.**

What Is the Language of the Heart?

It has long been recognized that people learn and process information differently. Some learn best by seeing visual demonstrations, while others need only to hear instruction to grasp knowledge. God knows you better than you know yourself and communicates with you in the way you need to hear it.

The language of your heart is how God speaks to you at the core of your being. Consistently recognizing His voice will require taking risks and testing it out in faith. If you sense God speaking to you, write it in your journal. Then see if what you hear aligns with the truth in the Scriptures. If it does, act on it to test if it's really God. As you step out in faith, realise that you will make mistakes. Don't give up, but adopt a growth mindset. Seek to be mentored by someone who is more spiritually mature in this area and can help you learn from your mistakes and fine-tune your discernment and hearing.[22]

Here are some common ways God may communicate with you:

- visually (through images, visions, dreams)
- scriptures
- words (for example, thoughts)
- impressions (which is also called intuitive knowing)
- feelings (emotions)
- body sensations

The truth is that God is always communicating with us, but we don't recognize it as Him. Our tendency is to edit what we hear and write it off as our own imagination or wishful thinking, especially if He is speaking kind words to us. We assume that God will tell us what's wrong with us but not what He loves about us. That level of intimacy makes us uncomfortable, so we often reject it.

As you get to know God more and learn to engage your own heart and embrace your uniqueness, you will be invited to take deliberate steps to guard your heart so the truth can become deeply embedded, forming an unshakeable foundation.

There are five ways in which you can begin to connect with your own heart and express love towards the real you.

1. Honour your heart. This involves listening to what your heart tells you, paying attention to the signals of your heart, and taking time to consider what it may be communicating. This demonstrates worth and value. Share what you discover with a mentor or trusted friend.

2. Take care of your soul. Taking care of yourself is something you can do daily to express love for yourself. Eating healthy, getting exercise, going for a massage, or simply incorporating rest into your lifestyle are all good ways of caring for yourself. Listen to inspirational music, surround yourself with positive people, and never put yourself down. The book of Jude says that as your soul prospers, so will the rest of your life.

Your soul contains your heart, your place of thinking, feeling, and choosing. Intentionally removing from your heart all that is toxic, tormenting, or rooted in lies is an important part of watching over your soul and keeping it pure. Most people don't realize that the enemy wants us to hang on to things that aren't ours to carry, nor healthy for our soul. These things include other people's pain, violating images, and offenses. These serve to clutter the soul and block our ability to discern the voice of God.

3. Engage in meaningful touch. Dr. Colbert believes that "one of the foremost ways you can love yourself is to care for your skin. The way you treat your skin—and the way you allow others to touch you, literally and figuratively—is a great indicator of health."[23] The way you respond to touch will indicate how much you love yourself. If you have a healthy love for yourself, you will enjoy being touched or hugged by others in meaningful and appropriate ways. The opposite is also true. If you have a healthy self-love, you will reach out and touch others with hugs and in other healthy, godly ways.

4. Live with integrity. The true meaning of integrity is living in a way that's consistent with who you are and what you value. Living according to your values includes ordering your days and managing your time so that you can focus on the tasks and relationships that are of highest priority.

Just because your phone is buzzing doesn't mean you need to answer it right away. I have periods of my day called "bubble time," periods when I don't check emails or answer phone calls. I simply focus on my other priorities.

Being the same person in public as you are in private is another indicator of integrity.

Ultimately, you will know how much you are living in integrity. Zig Ziglar said, "You cannot consistently perform in a manner that is inconsistent with the way you see yourself."[24] Eventually, your beliefs will show up in your actions. The sooner your actions are aligned to who you are and what you value, the sooner you will experience inner peace, a clear conscience, and greater fulfillment.

5. Journal your journey. In the technologically advanced, fast-paced world we live in, cultivating your heart and nurturing your soul requires deliberate action and focus. A very simple way to love and honour yourself is taking time to journal your thoughts, feelings, and questions as you engage in the transformation process. This gives you a place to express your heart fully, without editing, and to reflect on what comes up in your heart on any given day. Create the space to listen and connect with your heart. At the same time, journaling is a great way to record the words and ways God speaks to you as you take time to listen.

Stepping Forward

- In what ways have you honoured your heart this week? What was the result?
- Are you open to being touched by others emotionally, spiritually, and physically (appropriately)?

- Are you willing to express your own emotions authentically? If not, then why not? What will it cost you if you don't?
- How different would your life and relationships be if you truly loved yourself?
- Journal your discoveries.

Endnotes

15 Dr. Pearsall was a licensed neuropsychologist and clinical professor at the University of Hawai'i up until his death in 2007.

16 Dr. Don Colbert, *Deadly Emotions* (Wheaton, IL: Tyndale House, 2003), 88.

17 Ibid., 89.

18 Ibid.

19 Archibald D. Hart, *The Bible for Hope: Caring for People God's Way* (Nashville, TN: Thomas Nelson, 2001), 961.

20 Colbert, *Deadly Emotions*, 90.

21 Ibid.

22 For a more in-depth teaching on how God speaks to his children, see: Mark and Patti Virkler, *4 Keys to Hearing God's Voice* (Shippensburg, PA: Destiny Image, 2001).

23 Colbert, *Deadly Emotions*, 212.

24 Zig Ziglar, "The Way You See Yourself," *Ziglar.com*. Date of access: June 25, 2018 (https://www.ziglar.com/quotes/you-cannot-perform-manner/). See: Zig Ziglar, *Better than Good: Creating a Life You Can't Wait to Live* (Nashville, TN: W Publishing Group, 2007).

chapter four

Meaningful Connections with Others

...love one another fervently from a pure heart.

—1 Peter 1:22, AMPC

Relationships are the place where we get hurt, and also the place where we receive healing. The very place you want to avoid is the place where you will also experience the greatest joy and restoration. How you interact with people in your life will either add value to them or take something away from them.

I am constantly challenged by these words, which the apostle Paul wrote to the Roman Christians: *"Owe nothing to anyone—except for your obligation to love one another. If you love your neighbor, you will fulfill the requirements of God's law"* (Romans 13:8).

Believing you are meant to be a gift to the people around you is vital if you are to embrace your uniqueness and fulfill your divine purpose. Offering who you are to the world means reaching out to connect with others in meaningful ways to give out of what you have been given.

The Scriptures tell us that you can comfort others with the same comfort you received from God. As you yield to God as your source, your life will undergo a process of transformation. Even in the early stages of that process, you will find that some people around you will be inspired and desire to experience the freedom you're enjoying. You don't have to wait until you are perfect to be used by God. In fact, it is in your weakest moments, if your heart is yielded to Him, that His love and strength can flow through you most powerfully.

The late Jim Rohn, a famous motivational speaker, said that you're the average of the five people you most often hang around with.[25] Relationships are a normal and necessary part of life, and the quality of your relationships will determine the quality of your life. The more you understand the fullness of your identity in Christ, the more you will discover the real you and desire to share your faith with others who don't yet know God. When you learn to walk in the fullness of all you are created to be, people will naturally encounter God as they interact with you.

One of my favorite books is Robert E. Coleman's *The Master Plan of Evangelism*. In it, Coleman says,

> Evangelism is not an optional accessory to our life. It is the heartbeat of all that we are called to be and do. It is the commission of the church that gives meaning to all else that is undertaken in the name of Christ.[26]

Your relationship with Christ is personal, but it is not meant to be private. The closer you get to God, the more your desire grows to share that love relationship with those around you.

Connection with Others

In his book *The Seven Longings of the Human Heart*, Mike Bickle reminds us,

> Intimacy means so much more than a physical union. It is the empowering confidence people have in one another that allows them to share the deepest parts of their hearts—their hopes and dreams, their fears and failures, their feelings and frustrations.[27]

While human intimacy has its limits, intimacy with God is a never-ending adventure. As you deliberately seek to know God more, you will experience intimate expressions of His love that strengthen and fill you up. It is out of the overflow of this love relationship with him that your capacity to love others is expanded.

Our western societies have cheapened what was intended to be a powerful resource to stimulate creativity, passion, and transformational love. Even spirituality is reduced to feelings of impersonal energy flowing through your body and heightening your consciousness. But in my experience, spiritual connection isn't just about me becoming in tune with the universe and drawing energy from it to be my best self. God's original intent for my life is so much bigger than that.

> While human intimacy has its limits, intimacy with God is a never-ending adventure.

The God who created the universe is a personal, relational, and passionate lover. In fact, He *is* love personified! *God* and *love* are inseparable and synonymous. You and I are wired to demonstrate and radiate this love wherever we find ourselves. Becoming whole enables us to love each other more deeply from a pure heart. When the first humans chose to take life into their own hands, it severed not only their spiritual connection with God but also their heart connection with each other.

When God created Adam, the first human, He affirmed that they were wired for relationship: *"It is not good for the man to be alone"* (Genesis 2:18)—that is, it not good for someone to be without a human companion. You are not meant to do life alone, void of heart-centred relationships. I'm not saying you have to get married to experience this. You can learn to have intimate and pure friendships if you are willing to allow the real you to be known. This is part of what it means to *"love each other deeply with all your heart"* (1 Peter 1:22).

Engaging in Meaningful Connections

Have you ever had a phone conversation or Skype call that was hard to understand because of an unstable connection? You may have left the conversation wondering what you missed and what the caller had really meant to say. This can be frustrating, confusing, and even disheartening. How different would your life be if every interaction you had throughout your day left you feeling valued, strengthened, and inspired? What impact would you have on others if you left them feeling that way?

While attending graduate school, I shared an apartment with an international student named Keiko who had come to study at a theological college nearby. Keiko had become a Christian while attending college in her homeland of Japan. She had lived through years of rejection from her parents, who hadn't accepted her new faith. She'd lived in their house for two years following her conversion without having a single conversation with her dad. From his perspective, she had died.

The pain of such rejection propelled Keiko to pursue a more intimate relationship with God. She was the most authentic, loving, and spiritually healthy person I had ever met. Just being with her made me want to know God more deeply. She was a gift to me. God used her to teach me how to go beyond conversation to connection, for when she spoke or listened, her whole being reached out to connect. This transformed my own spiritual relationship and helped lay the foundation for how I relate to others today.

Leadership expert John C. Maxwell says that to really connect with someone requires you to be intentional and present to the person.[28] This involves not just an intellectual conversation, but a wholehearted exchange in which your spirit opens to embrace all that is being expressed to you.

It is important to remember, however, that authentic communication requires discernment as to how much and to whom you choose to open the deepest parts of your heart. Nevertheless, I believe it is possible to live in such a way that every person you interact with feels valued and loved. Keep in mind that your ability to love and connect with others will be determined by the degree with which you are able to, first of all, receive God's love and connect intimately with Him. Then, secondly, it is determined by your ability to engage your own heart.

In her book *How Did I Get So Busy?* Valorie Burton says that one-on-one connection is "the very foundation for a well-rounded, fulfilling life."[29] She goes on to say that "making a meaningful connection with the people you care about often means being pro-active."[30]

Establishing and nurturing the relationships that are most important to you will require creativity and intentional action. It's easy to go through life taking our friends and family for granted, drifting through life. I'm just as guilty of this as the next person. In the busyness of life, we somehow expect closeness to just automatically happen. It rarely does.

Worse yet, we often settle for superficial relationships believing that they're good enough. However, in my experience, whenever I stop growing in depth and intimacy in my human relationships, I am in danger of becoming apathetic and passive. Burton says that if you truly value a relationship, it will be necessary "to create the circumstances under which a relationship can flourish."[31]

She suggests developing certain habits that will help you reach out regularly to others and make heart-to-heart connections.

1. Engage in stimulating conversations. Initiate conversations with friends and family with a question such as, "What's the best thing that's happened to you today?" Stimulating conversations are ones where you refuse to allow your talk to become routine. It means not settling for the status quo or shallow exchanges, like talking about the weather or other superficial topics. Dare to go deeper as your relationships grow.

2. Reach out with hugs, kisses, and meaningful touch that nurture the soul. As a society, we have gone to the extreme in this area and deprived each other of even simple gestures, such as a hand on an arm or shoulder, in fear of being accused of being inappropriate. This has served to further starve us of an important element in cultivating meaningful connections. Physical touch is extremely powerful as a means to bring emotional healing to those closest to you. Beyond the physical, you can touch someone deeply by simply smiling, making eye contact, or speaking words of encouragement and acceptance. Proverbs 12:25 states that worry weighs a person down, and an encouraging word cheers a person up.

3. Help someone in need. Giving to others in meaningful ways, thus expressing love and value, creates connections. My late husband's parents, Darrell and Isabel Dewar, are great examples of connecting with people in this way. They are constantly giving of their time to help others in need. Mother Teresa's whole life was devoted to serving the needs of others in significant, life-changing ways. Whether helping a single mom with childcare, dropping off groceries for the elderly, calling a friend to let them know how much you appreciate them, or helping a child struggling with homework, there are many everyday ways in which you can make a meaningful connection with others.

4. Acknowledge people for who they are. People's assessment of their self-worth is often connected to their role, responsibilities, or anticipated rewards. Communicating acceptance and value to a person beyond what they do imparts strength, confidence, and feelings of love.

5. Laughing together. I have a number of friends who make me laugh easily every time we talk. Their light-hearted nature makes even routine tasks enjoyable. After my first husband died, I walked through a season of weeping and grief. During that time, I found my soul being nourished even after brief conversations with certain friends. Two of those friends were Jocelyne and Tricia. They loved to laugh. Just by being themselves, they often enabled me to return to joy, not as a distraction, but as a means of embracing the present and connecting with them. That is one of the many gifts they give to others. Laughter has a way of lifting off heaviness and creating close bonds between people.

Engaging wholeheartedly with others may make you feel vulnerable while at the same time allowing you to experience tremendous joy. The mixture of these emotions scares people and often confuses them as to the intent behind the interaction or purpose of the relationship. Heart-centred connections can be a powerful means to lift one's spirits, awaken one's soul, and ease the pain of one's suffering. Proverbs 15:30 echoes this truth: *"A cheerful look brings joy to the heart; good news makes for good health."* Connections become transformational the more you are willing to be real and to engage in wholehearted communication.

As you step forward to engage your heart and interact with others in meaningfully ways, you may find yourself reacting to certain situations and becoming aware of issues that are preventing you from connecting deeper. These reactions are often indicators of where your heart still needs freedom from beliefs that are contrary to God's truth. Embracing this process to wholeness and freedom is the subject of the next section of this book.

Stepping Forward

- What do you find most challenging about developing closer relationships?
- What one thing can you do this week to make a meaningful connection with someone in your life?
- Journal your discoveries.

Endnotes

25   Jim Rohn, "Quotable quote," *Goodreads*. Date of access: June 25, 2018 (https://www.goodreads.com/quotes/1798-you-are-the-average-of-the-five-people-you-spend).

26   Robert E. Coleman, *The Master Plan of Evangelism* (Grand Rapids, MI: Revell, 1993), 88.

27   Mike Bickle, *The Seven Longings of the Human Heart* (Kansas City, MO: Forerunner Media, 2006), 97.

28   John Maxwell, "Connecting Always Requires Energy," *JohnMaxwell.com*. September 27, 2009 (http://www.johnmaxwell.com/blog/connecting-always-requires-energy).

29   Valorie Burton, *How Did I Get So Busy?* (Colorado Springs, CO: Waterbrook Press, 2007), 63.

30   Ibid.

31   Ibid., 65.

Key #2

EMBRACE THE PROCESS

———————

But whenever someone turns to the Lord, the veil is taken away. For the Lord is the Spirit, and wherever the Spirit of the Lord is, there is freedom. So all of us who have had that veil removed can see and reflect the glory of the Lord. And the Lord—who is the Spirit—makes us more and more like him as we are changed into his glorious image.

—2 Corinthians 3:16–18

chapter five

Change Is Your Friend

If you plan to keep step with Jesus the Pioneer, you better expect some changes.[32]

—Erwin McManus

Have you ever attended a high school reunion and noticed how much certain people change over the years? Some people experience more dramatic changes than others. For example, one of my older brothers, Leo, was the shortest guy in his class when he graduated. Several years later at his high school reunion, his former classmates were surprised to see that he was taller than all of them. His biggest growth spurt happened after high school. These changes were physical and most noticeable, but some people can go year after year and never change in their mindset or attitudes—and they wonder why their life is going in circles.

There is an engagement process in which God invites each of His children to undergo transformation and ongoing change. At one time, I was afraid of change because I associated change with words like *unpredictable, chaotic,* and *out of control.* However, I discovered along the way that intentional change is actually normal and a necessary ingredient to becoming whole and living the real me. Today, I approach change as a friend and welcome it as a catalyst to propel me forward to live out my purpose. The book of Romans 12:2 instructs,

> *Don't copy the behavior and customs of this world, but let God transform you into a new person by changing the way you think. Then you will learn to know God's will for you, which is good and pleasing and perfect.*

You may be like most people and fear that the "new person" in this verse might be somebody you don't want to be; in fact, it's the real you that your heart is searching for.

Change is something everyone has to face, and in fact it's one of the few constants one can expect in life. Where there is no change, there is no life. Physiologically, change happens without your conscious awareness. Your skin and hair are constantly in regeneration mode. Research says that approximately every thirty-five days, your body develops a whole new layer of skin cells. From the moment you are conceived until your death, your body experiences ongoing and spontaneous change.

Spiritual change is different. Instead of being automatic, it requires intentional focus and choice. Spiritual growth, expansion, and maturity will only happen to the degree to which you are willing to let the truth of God seep through the soil of your heart and become firmly rooted.

As it is with a tall tree, spiritual maturity and strong character require internal development or growth before you can see fruit and strength on the outside. Some plants are stunted because their root systems keep them in a dwarf state. When your spiritual growth is stunted, you feel frustrated and unable to break through to what you perceive to be possible.

But when it comes to spiritual growth, your growth isn't just stunted. If you aren't moving forward and growing, you're actually going backwards.

Author Valorie Burton once wrote, "Change doesn't have to be difficult. It does, however, need to be intentional."[33] Stepping forward and living true to who you were made to be will require that you learn to embrace the process of transformation. This will involve a willingness to trust and a commitment to not give up. We'll discuss this further in a later chapter, but for now let's look at the nature of change.

Understanding Change

In the modern era, our culture is experiencing exponential growth in almost every sector of society, especially in the areas of information and technology. According to Norman W. Edmund, a researcher who investigates the application of the scientific method, by 2020 the amount of knowledge in the world is projected to double every 73 days.[34] As a consequence, whole new systems of communicating and learning will be required for us to cope with it.

The late Howard Hendricks, author of *Color Outside the Lines*, said, "Change is not just a cultural fact, it's a biblical fact, too."[35] This is confirmed by such passages as Romans 8:29, which teaches that we are *"predestined to become conformed to the image of His Son"* (NASB). Indeed, if it is part of your original design to reflect the nature of Christ, then isn't it reasonable to expect change to be a normal part of your journey? Speaker Leo Buscaglia believes that

> every day you should be seeing the world in a new and personal way. The tree outside your house is no longer the same, so look at it. Your husband, wife, child, mother, and father are changing daily, so look at them. Everything is in the process of change, including you.[36]

Hendricks pointed out that if organizations want to survive, they need to embrace change and creativity to remain relevant to the people within their reach. He affirms that some things are non-negotiable and form the bedrock upon which we stand as we navigate life. Even though the message of the gospel is unchanging, its effect on people who accept it is transformational. In fact, it provokes such profound changes that individual lives, communities, and even whole people groups are significantly impacted.

Transformation is the outcome a caterpillar experiences as it goes through the cocooning process, eventually emerging to take flight as a butterfly. The freedom to fly came about as the caterpillar embraced who it was designed to be and trusted the process. As a result, it developed brilliantly coloured wings in the dark and hidden cocoon and emerged free and complete.

This process, which is necessary for the butterfly, is just as critical to your life, emotionally and spiritually. Most people try to take shortcuts to reach their goals faster. This can be both detrimental and counterproductive.

During one of my family's visits to the Calgary Zoo, we became awed by the butterfly room. Butterflies of various sizes and colours were flying all around. Behind glass enclosures were cocoons at different stages of metamorphosis. It was fascinating to see the live display and be reminded of how important it is to let the transformation process run its full course.

Recent advancements in ultrasound technology make it possible for us to see clearly that a baby in the mother's womb is actually a human being and contains the needed DNA from the point of conception. The process of shaping and forming, of development and growth, that happens inside the womb is essential so that the baby can be equipped to experience the fullness of the life she or he was designed to live outside the womb. Even writing this book was a process, progressing from a thought and an idea in my heart to the finished product. Seasons, too, are distinguished by changes. All life is about process and change. The sooner you learn to accept change as your friend, the sooner you will be able to enjoy the freedom that change produces.

My Personal Transformation

Unexpected events in 2007 started me on a process of another kind, one of making sense out of unanswered prayers and re-creating my future. After being married to my first husband, Darwin, for more than seventeen years, he was diagnosed with a brain tumour and died within three months. That kind of change is never welcome. After his death, my three children and I began to walk through a process of grieving, healing, and creating a new normal. For some people, the loss of a loved one can bring about an identity crisis that makes the recovery time much darker and longer. I didn't experience this kind of crisis at the time, but I did many years earlier.

My late teens and early twenties were significant times for me both spiritually and emotionally. That's when I first experienced the healing power of God's truth and love. I had grown up not trusting anyone except my mom, so I never really felt safe. My home environment had been chaotic and confusing with an alcoholic father who would become violent and angry every time he drank.

From a young age, my heart was filled with pain and bitterness, and I was tormented by fears. In my struggle to survive, I took control of what I could, which led to me becoming anorexic. I closed my heart off and didn't trust anyone.

Trust was one of the first foundations God rebuilt in my life. As a result, I grew to know and trust Him as my loving Father. I came to discover my identity in Christ and started loving who I was, embracing my unique strengths, value, and worth.

This is probably why I didn't go into despair when Darwin died. Did I grieve? Absolutely! Did I have sorrow and pain? Enormously! But in the midst of all the grief and sorrow, there resided an incredible peace and strength knowing that God was with me. Even though my future was going to look different, who I was at the core hadn't changed. My identity and life purpose remained the same.

I was grateful for the mentors who had influenced me years earlier and taught me the importance of embracing change and transformation; my life had been established on a foundation that was now unshakeable. My life was rooted and grounded in His love. This foundation was established step by step as I learned to embrace the changes that lay before me and cooperate with the work of the Holy Spirit.

It is this same kind of process that I encourage you to embrace.

Why People Resist Change

As you step forward to live in freedom and wholeness, you will experience some resistance to the changes you're making. Some of the resistance may come from within you and some may come from family members and friends. It's important to be ready for this opposition so that you can prepare yourself to deal with it.

Part of your preparation will involve understanding why people resist change. The first area in which you'll experience resistance is inside you. When something threatens to upset your comfort zone or what you believe to be true in your heart, you will resist. You will try to maintain your life the way it is, but this will work against you when you're trying to step forward to establish new and healthy disciplines. Whatever you previously established as normal, the mind and heart work to maintain that, even if that normal is destructive or unhealthy.

There are three common reasons why people resist change.

1. Change taps into fear. If you don't understand how change works, it will trigger fear in your heart, and you'll struggle to pull yourself back. Also, whenever a person changes it affects people around them. Even small and seemingly insignificant changes can create this ripple effect. Sometimes family and friends will react to a decision you make, even if it's a good decision. They may fear how it will change how you relate to them, how it will interfere with how much time you spend with them. Others may fear a loss of control when you make changes that are independent of them, such as with a parent whose child has reached adulthood. Still others will react in jealousy, fearing that you will consider them to be less important as you move forward.

2. Change challenges people's mindsets. Many people view change as negative, and they resist change because of this. Opportunities to change can expose one's underlying belief system, revealing anything that is faulty. People may resist change because they fear the unknown and want to control the process. They may believe that because the steps and outcome are uncertain, it can't be right. Instead of trusting God, they get stuck in their need to understand and control things. Their view of life may be challenged, which sometimes leads them to be offended as they perceive the changes to be a judgment on their intelligence. Of course, this can tap into pride and a variety of other limiting beliefs.

To successfully navigate change, you need to be open to shift your attitudes and perspective, and leave room for new possibilities beyond your understanding.

3. Change disrupts the comfort zone. As mentioned earlier, the brain is wired to keep us in a state of homeostasis. Many people don't move forward because they simply get too comfortable in their situation and surroundings. They live by the mantra, "If it's uncomfortable, it can't be good." What they don't realize is that the comfort zone is only intended to be a temporary resting spot, not a place to set up permanent residence, before moving to the next step.

In his book *The Barbarian Way*, Erwin McManus wrote that a person's walk with God should not be about looking to Him to create for us a safe and comfortable life, but instead to create in us a heart that is willing to go wherever He leads and do whatever He asks, thus allowing us to fulfill our unique calling on the earth.

Although God brings peace, He doesn't aim to sedate you. Even though He brings you comfort, His goal is not to make you comfortable. McManus put it succinctly when he wrote that God's purpose is to "awaken your spirit to be truly alive."[37] You will discover that true growth happens only when you dare to step out of your comfort zone and into the unknown, trusting God with the process.

The Benefits of Change

You may not see why change is necessary, and it may take time, trust, and testing to convince you otherwise. If you're willing to learn, you will discover that the rewards of embracing change far outweigh the risks.

Here are four of the most important benefits for you to consider. This isn't an exhaustive list, and I encourage you to add to it as you experience your own rewards for embracing change as your friend.

> By embracing ongoing growth and change, you are embracing life itself.

1. Change produces ongoing growth. In my office sits a framed quote by Winkie Pratney, who is a speaker and author from New Zealand. The quote simply says, "If you stop learning, you stop your pursuit of God." Embracing change is absolutely essential if you're committed to a lifestyle of growth and learning. You will notice that as your attitude and approach to change shifts, you will feel emotionally and spiritually stronger as well as physically healthier.

Journeying with God is all about change and adventure. When you connect to His heart, you give Him permission to align your way of thinking to His and train you to live in such a way that you offer the real you to the world every day. What got you this far in life won't get you to the next level. To embrace change is to make room in your heart for His truth to be received, your mind to be renewed, your true identity to be revealed, and your unique purpose to be released. McManus says it this way: "You cannot meet the Creator of the universe and remain the same."[38] By embracing ongoing growth and change, you are embracing life itself.

If you've ever read biographies of successful people, you will probably have noticed certain qualities they have in common. One of these common traits is having a resilient spirit. Several years ago, I was invited to write a chapter in a book edited by Sheri Keys, *Smart Women Live Their Why*. In my chapter, I listed resilience as one of the keys to successfully navigating change.

> Resilience is defined as the power or ability to return to the original form, position, or state after being bent, compressed, or stretched. It's like having elasticity. In her most recent book *Where Will You Go from Here?* Valorie Burton discusses the quality of resilience thoroughly. She said, "The essence of resilience is your ability to effectively navigate adversity and courageously face whatever life throws your way. Though you may be bruised and battered by challenges, your spirit still soars."[39]
>
> Undergirding resilience is the belief that you can overcome any experience and that the experience can actually make you a better person. It is seeing obstacles as opportunities to grow. In her book, Burton relates resilience to tempered glass, which is glass that is made stronger due to repeated exposure to heat and cold. She cites one definition of *temper* as a means to make stronger and more resilient through hardship.[40]

Resilient people know that the process of change is just as important, if not more important, than the outcome. In the heat of battle, your character gets tested and you become stronger, allowing you to emerge victoriously with even more to offer the world. By embracing change, you experience personal growth and the expansion of your inner capacity.

2. Change strengthens relationships. Marriages fail for many reasons, but the most common reason is the unwillingness of one or both spouses to change. Your focus is often on trying to change the other person when, in fact, your relationship would drastically improve if you focused more on allowing God to heal your heart and change the way you think.

Taking responsibility for the condition of your own heart tells others that you love them. You want to give of your best self even if that means enduring potentially painful processes of change and transformation. Why settle for a mediocre relationship when you can have a richer, more fulfilling one?

Developing stronger relationships will require a commitment to embrace change and to take responsibility for your own stuff, and to engage in the process of transformation for as long as it takes. My life is proof that this is possible. Everything in my childhood environment predicted that I would grow up to have unhealthy boundaries and toxic relationships. This would have been my story if I hadn't encountered the love of Jesus as a teenager and had mentors in my life who loved me enough to not let me settle for anything less than the wholeness and freedom Jesus died to give me.

3. Changes fulfills your unique purpose. Jesus laid down His position in heaven to fulfill His purpose on the earth. Talk about embracing change! In fact, it was His understanding of the bigger picture that allowed Him to endure painful circumstances and eventual death, knowing that the changes were necessary to fulfill His unique purpose and restore mankind. In the J.B. Phillips translation of the New Testament, Hebrews 12:2 says, *"For he himself endured a cross and thought nothing of its shame because of the joy he knew would follow his suffering"* (Phillips).

With His eyes fixed on the goal, He embraced the process of testing, trials, and transformation. His life changed from being a carpenter to a travelling preacher. He left his humble beginnings and family in Nazareth and challenged the political and religious mindsets of His day. The Scriptures reveal that Jesus learned obedience by the things He suffered. This implies a process that served to prepare Him to carry out His divine mission. His decisions impacted not just His generation but lives all over the world today. He chose obedience and submission every step of the way! As a result, He became the ultimate change agent, fulfilling His purpose on the earth, and He invites us to do the same.

4. Change glorifies God. Embracing change means ultimately saying, "I am not perfect. God knows me better than I know myself, so I choose to trust Him for the process that's necessary to release me to live the *real me*." The Westminster shorter catechism states that mankind's ultimate mission in life is "to glorify God, and to enjoy him forever."[41] Exactly how you do that is your unique mission. God is glorified when we embrace life and acknowledge that we cannot bring about the growth on our own. John 6:63 says, *"Human effort accomplishes nothing."*

Many people are dissatisfied with their lives and know they want change, but they don't know where to start. Perhaps that's where you find yourself today. If you want your circumstances to change, the change needs to start with you. As you seek to know Jesus more, I believe that your desires will shift and you will want to live the way Jesus said was possible. As you choose to accept Hs truth, transformation happens within you, which causes others to change around you. As you engage in healthy and positive change, you cause others around you to follow. The Holy Spirit within you is the true agent of change in and through you. I agree with McManus when he said, "Evolution of man is not the key to humanity's freedom; transformation is."[42]

In 2 Corinthians 3:18, we are told, *"And the Lord—who is the Spirit—makes us more and more like him as we are changed into his glorious image."* This clearly explains that embracing the process of transformation is key to reflecting God to the world.

When you embrace the processes of life, no matter how difficult they may seem, God is glorified as others see you come through stronger and with more freedom than before. Staying connected to Him empowers you to make the necessary shifts in your mind and heart as you navigate the changes. You were made for intimacy and to radiate the true character and nature of your Creator. As you submit to the work of the Holy Spirit within you, you will be healed and your heart will become free. You will find that people are attracted to His presence in you.

Stepping Forward

- What change are you resisting?
- In what ways are you experiencing resistance from others regarding the change you want to make?
- What will it cost you if you make the change? What will it cost you if you don't?
- What step can you take today to move you closer to living the real you?
- Journal your discoveries.

Endnotes

32   Erwin McManus, *The Barbarian Way*, 53.

33   Burton, *How Did I Get So Busy?* 64.

34 Jason S. Wrench, *Workplace Communication for the 21st Century: Tools and Strategies that Impact the Bottom Line, Volume One* (Santa Barbara, CA: ABC-CLIO Publisher, 2013), 1.

35 Howard Hendricks, *Color Outside the Lines* (Nashville, TN: W Publishing Group, 1998), 10.

36 Ibid., 175.

37 McManus, *The Barbarian Way*, 66.

38 Ibid., 65.

39 Valorie Burton, *Where Will You Go from Here?* (Colorado Springs, CO: Waterbrook Press, 2011), 6.

40 Sheri Keys, ed., *Smart Women Live Their Why: Why Women Entrepreneurs Are Living on Purpose and in Passion* (Deadwood, OR: Butterfly Women Press, 2011), 139.

41 "Westminster Short Catechism Project," *Shorter Catechism*. July 30, 2016 (http://www.shortercatechism.com/resources/wsc/wsc_001.html).

42 McManus, *The Barbarian Way*, 104.

chapter six

From Mess to Message

All problem-solving begins with a mess, that is, an ill-defined challenge.[43]
—Howard Hendricks

Let's face it: things were a mess when Jesus got arrested! The disciples scattered, feeling lost, confused, and afraid. Conversations between His closest followers probably included such comments as "What went wrong?" and "It wasn't supposed to turn out this way!" and "Why doesn't God just intervene?" Their master had been arrested, publicly humiliated, and taken to court. Was He really who He said He was? Confusion and shock flooded their senses. One of the disciples was so gripped with fear that he denied ever knowing Jesus.

From an observer's perspective, it seemed like a tragedy and a huge mess. However, from the big picture perspective, it was the unfolding of the greatest message of all time, a message that would go on to change lives and transform cultures. This developed into the most incredible story the world has ever known, and its impact is only increasing over time.

What about your life? Does it seem like a mess right now? Is it hard to see past the pain, betrayal, and loss? Well, the Holy Spirit is in the business of taking our mess and turning it into a message through which God is glorified and you are empowered. As you embrace the process one step at a time, you will begin to see your life story unfold in a way you never imagined possible.

God, who made the universe, is creative and innovative. He saw a formless, chaotic void and spoke order, beauty, and life into the random mess, producing countless inventions and masterpieces. He took dirt from the ground and fashioned a complex, sensitive human being who beautifully reflected Him. Jesus endured the cross with all its discomfort and pain for the hope that was promised on the other side of it. He was beaten, bullied, and severely mocked as punishment for our wrongdoings. This messy process is described in Isaiah 53:3–5:

> *He was despised and rejected—a man of sorrows, acquainted with deepest grief. We turned our backs on him and looked the other way. He was despised, and we did not care.*
>
> *Yet it was our weaknesses he carried; it was our sorrows that weighed him down. And we thought his troubles were a punishment from God, a punishment for his own sins! But he was pierced for our rebellion, crushed for our sins. He was beaten so we could be whole. He was whipped so we could be healed.*

When my first husband began his battle with an inoperable brain tumour, I fully trusted that God would bring him through and heal him completely. Yet I struggled with the process.

One day when my children were at school, I returned from the hospital early, feeling exhausted. I went into my living room, lay facedown on the rug, and began pouring out my heart. This time, instead of asking for healing, I cried out, "God, what are You doing? Where are You at work in this? I don't understand. Why are you not answering my prayer to heal him?"

After some time had passed, and I had finished releasing my anguish and pain, I saw a vision in my mind of Jesus on the cross, crying out to His Father, "Father, where are you? Why have you abandoned me?"

The possibility that Jesus had said these things wasn't a new revelation to me, but the feelings that accompanied those questions were. I found myself feeling what Jesus must have felt on the cross. Jesus had experienced loss of connection with His Father and seemed to wonder why He couldn't feel his Father's presence. It was as if I was one with Him and he was saying to me that He was one with me, sharing in my suffering as I was in His. He comforted me with the reminder that He knows the pain of feeling disconnected from the Father and from someone you love.

Immediately, my pain lifted and the anguish subsided. God was with me in the mess, bringing about His divine message through the situation. At that moment, I didn't know exactly what that message was going to be, but I knew that I could trust God to do it.

I thought about the many people who were being touched by Darwin as he interacted with the medical staff and others who came to visit him. His whole life had been lived in surrender to God, and countless people had come to know Jesus through him.

Even after his death, God continued to show me people whose lives had been transformed because Darwin had shared his faith with them. It was as if God had already let him in on a little secret when he spoke this scripture to his heart over and over, weeks before his death: *"I tell you the truth, unless a kernel of wheat is planted in the soil and dies, it remains alone. But its death will produce many new kernels—a plentiful harvest of new lives"* (John 12:24).

Trusting Beyond Understanding

Our human understanding will only take us so far. That's where faith begins, and we need to take a step forward to activate our ability to trust rather than figure it out intellectually.

After Darwin's death, I was confused and didn't understand. How was I going to explain this to my three young children? They would ask why God hadn't healed their daddy. During these times of grief and confusion, the enemy often tries to convince us that God isn't who He says He is, and that it's better to stop trusting in Him. This is where the reality of our faith is seen. We need to take action and submit our feelings to the Word of God to determine what is really true.

I decided to continue to believe the truth and stand firmly in it. As I searched the Scriptures to remind myself of the truth, I was drawn to a passage in John 21. Jesus had appeared to the disciples after the resurrection and warned Peter about the kind of death he would eventually experience. Peter asked whether John would also die prematurely. Jesus's responded, *"If I want him to remain until I return, what is that to you? As for you, follow me"* (John 21:22).

As difficult as it is to accept any kind of loss or sudden change in life, facing reality is key to moving forward. It is important to remember that God's ways are higher than our human ways. I don't believe that God caused Darwin's illness, nor do I fully understand the why and the how, yet I did have a choice whether to trust God in spite of the outcome.

My ability to trust God in this situation began years earlier with the decision that whenever I'd exhausted everything else I knew how to do, I would keep standing and continue to trust God's love and faithfulness. Your path is going to be different than mine, and neither path is more important than the other; they are of equal value and purpose. What is important is to keep your heart and mind fixed on what God is doing in and through your life as you embrace His processes.

The invitation to trust beyond my understanding has been a common thread throughout my life. I started out trusting very little, and at different points along the relationship, and in various ways, the Spirit of God invited me to step forward and apply Proverbs 3:5–6 to the situation: *"Trust in the Lord with all your heart; do not depend on your own understanding. Seek his will in all you do, and he will show you which path to take."* As I did, He came through and my trust muscles began to grow. Trust and faith is active, not passive, and it will require you to step forward beyond your understanding.

How to Overcome Feeling Overwhelmed

When you're in the centre of a messy situation, you may feel overwhelmed, even emotionally paralyzed and unsure about what to do next. The source of the struggle is often rooted in your need to be in control, yet you feel helpless and unable to dictate the process. Where once you felt confident, but now you may feel incompetent. Don't give up. As you focus your attention on God for the solution, humble your heart and lay down your need to control the process. You will receive the wisdom you need to make the next right step! This may require that you take a risk and go beyond your comfort zone and into the unknown.

Being content is not the same as being comfortable. You and I are meant to be content, which has to do with being at peace. So don't settle for comfort, but do be content.

Whenever we struggle to overcome something, it taps into issues of the heart. We can try to muster up the willpower and apply behaviour modification techniques, yet nothing changes until the beliefs of our hearts change. In the midst of the tension, take a moment and ask yourself, *What do I believe to be true about this situation? What do I believe will happen if I step out of my comfort zone?*

I once heard Jim Richards, a pastor and speaker, say that we all want the promise of God, but we don't want the

Nothing changes until the beliefs of our hearts change.

process He takes us through. When we're not willing to trust God for the process, and when we want to control the process, we resist change and feel overwhelmed. It's important to honour the process and not try to take shortcuts to ease our discomfort. Trust Him through the process, not just the promise.

As you do, making these four commitments will help you successfully navigate the journey and overcome any feelings of being overwhelmed you may feel.

1. Commit to seeking God. Change can often be overwhelming for people because they have their eyes and minds focused on the situation and its uncertainties. When this happens, it's beneficial to tune in and listen to your heart and to the Spirit of God for His perspective on whatever you 'e facing. Hebrews 4:16 serves to remind us, *"Let us then approach God's throne of grace with confidence, so that we may receive mercy and find grace to help us in our time of need."* This is an open invitation to connect with God whenever you need to, as often as you need to. As you run to Him, instead of away from Him, you will experience peace, creativity, and confidence to go through any circumstance.

Jesus also spoke of this open door policy:

Come to me, all of you who are weary and carry heavy burdens, and I will give you rest. Take my yoke upon you. Let me teach you, because I am humble and gentle at heart, and you will find rest for your souls. For my yoke is easy to bear, and the burden I give you is light.

—Matthew 11:28–30

I want to encourage you to not only believe in God but live in Him. Let Him share His heart with you and show you yours. The psalmist experienced the power of this when he complained about how those who don't serve God seemed to have all the blessings while he, who had been so faithful to God, was going through such painful times: *"Did I keep my heart pure for nothing? Did I keep myself innocent for no reason? I get nothing but trouble all day long; every morning brings me pain"* (Psalm 73:13–14).

Sound familiar? As he enquired of God for understanding, the psalmist not only discovered fresh perspective on the situation, but he also realized the unhealthy condition of his own heart and where he needed to change.

So I tried to understand why the wicked prosper. But what a difficult task it is! Then I went into your sanctuary, O God, and I finally understood the destiny of the wicked... Then I realized that my heart was bitter, and I was all torn up inside.

—Psalm 73:16–17, 21

As he stayed in God's presence, he became aware that relying on his own understanding alone had affected him emotionally and spiritually. Like the psalmist, we often stop short of overcoming a situation because we don't take the time to linger with God to see things from His perspective. Commit to seeking God in all your ways.

2. Commit to discovering the real you. In the midst of change, conflicts, and trials, knowing yourself can be the anchor you need to get through. Focusing on what you do know to be true rather than what you don't is essential to moving forward. As you discover the real you and learn to embrace your true identity, you will discover peace, clarity, and an increased ability to trust. You will be able to move forward with confidence in the truth that nothing can separate you from God's love. As you commit to knowing Christ more, you will also discover the real you.

3. Commit to responding and not reacting. Your response will determine your future. When you react negatively to change, it's usually because that change is touching an unresolved issue in your heart. It may tap into fears, insecurities, and painful memories. As these emotions surface, it will be important to acknowledge them and seek counsel as to the underlying issues triggering your reaction. If you choose to ignore the reactions and don't resolve the issues, you will be stuck and unable to move forward. Keep this truth in mind: it's not what happens to you that defines you but how you respond to what happens to you.[44]

4. Commit to growing through the process. Instead of seeing unexpected changes as obstacles, approach them as opportunities to grow, to understand yourself and others better, and to develop in character. Focus on seeing the nuggets of wisdom, knowledge, and truth you can take away from every situation. This often means being coachable and willing to allow your perspectives and attitudes to be challenged, and for more layers of your soul to be laid bare. Erwin McManus, author of *The Barbarian Way*, said, "If the God who is all-powerful, all-knowing, and all-present comes to dwell within your soul, you would expect at least some minor disruption."[45]

Make a decision today to approach trials and obstacles with courage and determination instead of fear. As you step into the unknown, pushing through the discomfort and embracing the work of the Holy Spirit, you will become more fully alive.

Pushing through discomfort with determination can be likened to an airplane at takeoff. Most of an airplane's fuel is consumed in the first few minutes as it lifts off and aims to reach a certain altitude. The force required for the airplane to fly against gravity and push through the sound barrier produces tremendous pressure inside the cabin, often causing the plane to shake. However, once the plane gets through that discomfort zone, flying is smoother and less fuel is needed to maintain equilibrium.

Our lives are similar. Pushing through the initial stages of change often requires more energy. This is why taking the first step often seems to be the hardest. However, if you persist and don't give up you will discover increased confidence and strength to live in wholeness and freedom, and an increased ability to go beyond what you previously thought possible.

The book of James serves as a great reminder of the rewards we can receive from seeing trials as opportunities to grow.

> *Consider it pure joy, my brothers and sisters, whenever you face trials of many kinds, because you know that the testing of your faith produces perseverance. Let perseverance finish its work so that you may* be mature and complete, not lacking anything.
>
> —James 1:2–4, NIV (emphasis added)

Whatever messy situation you may be facing, believe that God is good and can turn your mess into a masterpiece—if you choose to trust Him every step of the way. Don't just decide to *get* through the difficulties; make a commitment to *grow* through them and watch your life take on new meaning and fulfillment.

Stepping Forward

- In what areas of your life do you need to apply Proverbs 3:5–6?
- What scares you the most about trusting beyond your understanding?
- In what area do you need to trust in what you know to be true and not in what you don't know?
- Journal about what happens as you step forward and trust.
- Journal your discoveries.

Endnotes

43 Howard Hendricks, *Color Outside the Lines: A Revolutionary Approach to Creative Leadership* (Nashville, TN: W Publishing Group, 1998), 99.

44 The importance of making this commitment will be discussed in greater detail in a later chapter.

45 McManus, *The Barbarian Way*, 66.

chapter seven

Restoring Foundations

The foundations of law and order have collapsed. What can the righteous do?
—Psalm 11:3

In a world of fast food, turbo technology, and microwave mindsets, you may be struggling to understand why you need to endure a process and why you can't just have the quick fix.

Everything in life involves process. You may not recognize many of the processes you embrace every day because they've become second nature and automatic, such as tying your shoes and driving your car. Take driving a car, for example. Your first lesson behind the wheel may have seemed overwhelming and awkward because of all the new things you had to learn. After lots of practice, though, you felt more comfortable behind the wheel, and before long the process became so automatic that you hardly had to think about what to do next. The process established a pattern of thinking and systems of action that moved you forward.

Taking shortcuts in learning may get you to a result faster, but what essential tools, skills and treasures did you miss out on because you wanted the end result right now? No matter the process God initiates, He invites you to partner with Him as His Spirit works to achieve three goals: restoring true foundation, releasing the real you, and radiating His glory.

We'll look more closely at these three areas and how He accomplishes each, but in this chapter we'll just focus on the first area.

True Foundations

Friends in the construction industry once told me that the largest portion of their budget is spent on laying the foundation, no matter the size of the building. Why does something that is mostly hidden and out of sight cost so much? The reason is that it's designed to hold the weight of the rest of the structure and keep it standing strong for years to come. A faulty foundation is unstable and dangerous.

As it is in the natural sense, so it is for the spiritual foundation of your life.

The life Jesus came to bring isn't so much about the accumulation of material possessions and financial wealth; it has more to do with laying a foundation in your life that provides the strength, stability, and power to release you to accomplish your unique calling. This often means removing things such as limiting beliefs, distorted perceptions, and unresolved pain and replacing them with truth, forgiveness, trust, and intimate love.

God's Word is designed to help you build a strong and firm foundation in your life. It teaches us what is right and makes us realize what is wrong (2 Timothy 3:16). It corrects, equips, and prepares us to do His will.

As you come to know God and grow deeper in your relationship, He seeks to establish strong foundations in your life so that no matter what comes your way, you will remain standing and grow through it. Jesus spoke about this concept when He taught about the importance of not just hearing what God has to say, but practically applying it to your life (Luke 6:46–48). In other words, when you listen to God's instructions and put them into practice, you partner with Him to establish the necessary foundations in your life.

Wayne Cordeiro, pastor of New Hope Christian Fellowship in Hawaii, once told a story during a sermon about a time when a company hired a contractor to prepare a piece of land on which to build a house. The contractor was supposed to rip up the soil and remove the vegetation growing there, but because he was so busy he simply turned over the vegetation and added soil on top of it. Eventually, air pockets developed as the vegetation underneath started to decay, and the whole hillside collapsed, along with the new houses.

We are often just like that contractor. We use the excuse of being too busy to do the things that are necessary. Instead of removing the elements that might contaminate our hearts or cause the foundation of our lives to become shaky, such as anger, sexual immorality, pride, or lying, we ignore them and try to take shortcuts. Neglecting the process will prove to be a detrimental mistake.

Embracing the process involves believing that change can be a catalyst to creating the kind of life you desire and trusting that God knows what He's doing. It involves being open to letting Him transform your life, and letting Him guide you through the process in the way that is best for you and according to His original intention for your life. Think of it as having your very own personal coach training you to perform at your maximum capacity! If that's what you want, it's essential to let Him reveal the faulty habits or limiting beliefs that threaten to collapse the life you have been building through your own efforts.

Unlike most of the physical changes we undergo, changes at the heart level require us to make deliberate choices. Whenever we encounter ideas, perspectives, and even personalities that are different from our own, we can get offended—or at the very least, challenged. This discomfort often provides a clue to an area where God wants to adjust you belief system. Too often when situations are uncomfortable or awkward, we want to turn the other way and disconnect or resist. In my experience, however, these are the very times we need to stop, engage our hearts, and tune our spirits to listen to the Holy Spirit. Embracing the process means being willing to see ongoing growth as necessary, a gift designed to move you from where you are today to where you need to be in order to live the real you with freedom and wholeness.

In ancient Hebrew, there are twelve words that refer to a foundation. Psalm 11:3 talks about the importance of having a foundation that will endure the test of time. The foundation of most developed countries is a moral, political, economic, social, and spiritual society that brings stability to people's lives. But what if all these systems collapse and are ruined? What then? What will the righteous do? Indeed, the world has experienced tremendous instability in recent years. How has that impacted our hearts?

There is a phenomenon in nature called the "sinkhole effect" whereby everything looks good on the surface, but in reality the ground isn't solid underneath. In fact, it's ready to collapse at any moment. This describes the state of most people's lives. When the pressures of life come to bear, a person's true character is revealed and the gaps in their spiritual and emotional foundation become visible. In Psalm 11, the psalmist declares that he trusts in the Lord for protection, so why would anyone suggest that he seek safety in anything else, especially since everything around him is collapsing? He then concludes the psalm by saying, *"For the righteous Lord loves justice. The virtuous will see his face"* (Psalm 11:7).

This passage is as relevant today as it was the day it was written. Perhaps you're one of the many who feel hopeless and wearied by the state of the world. You may know where you need to go, but you don't know how to get there or whom to trust. The internal structures God wants you to have are strong enough to withstand the unexpected trials or storms of life. Even when circumstances leave you shaken to the core, the foundation of your life will not crumble if it's built on God's truth.

Before a proper foundation can be laid, garbage and debris must be removed, the soil examined for contaminants, and the environment cleansed of anything that could threaten to erode the new structure. This is part of what He is accomplishing as you embrace the process. It can be painful when He has to dig deep, but remember that the deeper the foundation, the stronger the structure is above ground, and the higher the building can rise. This is how He expands our capacity to carry and express more of his Heart.

In the years following my first husband's death, many people asked me if I felt lonely. I can honestly say that I did not. Did I have times when I missed him and missed being able to connect with him? Absolutely. Did I experience dark days of overwhelming grief and sorrow? Yes, lots of them. But I did not feel loneliness. Really! I'm being totally honest here. To me, loneliness implies a void of belonging. Based on this definition, I did not feel lonely, even though I was alone and without a human companion.

Many years ago, God began a process in my life that formed the foundation of my identity. He began to forge in me the ability to trust Him as my ultimate source of life and love. This season of loss was yet another opportunity to experience and echo this truth that *"[all] my fountains are in you"* (Psalm 87:7, NIV). Or as it says in the New Living Translation, *"The source of my life springs from Jerusalem!"*

As a young teenager, I chose to trust Him with my life. I invited Him to live in the deepest parts of my heart. At the onset of our marriage, as husband and wife, we declared to each other that God would be the centre of our lives and our number one source of fulfillment. We didn't say that church activities or ministry work would be number one, but rather our intimate connection with God. Our relationship with Him would be the only relationship above our marriage. Out of this place, drawing from Him as our source of love, we were able to love each other and create a solid marriage.

So Darwin's death did not change the fact that my ultimate source of fulfillment and life flowed from my relationship with God. I realize that I run the risk of being misunderstood here, but it's so essential in terms of understanding why it's so key to embrace the process in fulfilling your calling.

Although I missed experiencing my human connection with Darwin in profound ways, my deep place of feeling valued, loved, and complete was undisturbed. My identity—the person I saw myself as—had been established on God's truth through an earlier process, and it was still intact. As you seek to move forward to live true to how God made you, it's important to allow Him to establish the necessary foundation in your life that will prepare you for whatever lies ahead.

Elements of a Strong Foundation

There are four primary elements that make up a strong and healthy foundation in your spiritual connection with God. Let's touch on each one separately.

Foundation of Truth

A few years into our marriage, I purchased an antique side table. When my husband asked me how much I'd paid for it, I told a white lie. Do you know what kind of lie that is? It's the kind of lie that only tells half of the truth.

"It was on sale and I got a really good deal," I said.

For the sake of illustration, let's say the price was $125 and I got thirty percent off, making the final sale price $87.50. However, I had actually paid $125, which *was* the discounted price. My wording led him to believe that I had paid less than I had. I feared what he would say if I told him the complete truth.

God wouldn't let me get away with that, even though I had seen that sort of behaviour modelled for me while growing up.

That evening, I went to church for a prayer meeting.[46] While trying to pray, I kept seeing an image in my mind of me sitting on a wooden bench in a beautiful garden, enjoying the flowers. When I asked God what this meant, He showed me the even more beautiful garden behind me; it had all kinds of sweet-scented roses and other fragrant trees and flowers.

And my husband was there. I immediately knew what the dream meant. I had turned my back on what God had planned for me, and as a result I was enjoying only a small measure of the beautiful relationship He desired me to have in my marriage. My lie had resulted in a disconnection with my spouse. I asked God to forgive me and to uproot whatever had motivated me to lie.

When I returned home, I told my husband the truth and we prayed together for any seeds of deception to be uprooted.

My parents' relationship was such that my dad would get angry over simple things, and he often left my mom with very little money to buy food for the family. To avoid conflict, my mom was afraid to tell him how much she spent on groceries and essentials. That was one of the fears that took root in my heart, and for no logical reason it had sprung up that day, leading me to lie even though I had no reason to fear.

God used this incident to lead me along a process to establish an even stronger and deeper foundation of truth in my heart. To help me understand what He was trying to accomplish in that season, He highlighted Psalm 51:6 for me: *"But you desire honesty from the womb, teaching me wisdom even there."* He wasn't satisfied with mere words of truth; he was more interested in what was in the heart, where subtle deceptions can lay hidden and cause corruption if left unearthed.

An oft-quoted passage on the topic of truth can be found in John 8:32: *"And you will know the truth, and the truth will set you free."* When I looked up the meaning of the word truth in the original Greek, I discovered that it refers to "unveiled reality." This means that exposing true reality leads to freedom.

Once I became aware of the condition of my heart and the potential for it to be damaged by my lies, and once I realized what God was doing, I was free to choose another way to respond. Awareness is the first step to change and to walking in wholeness and freedom.

Foundation of Identity

As you step forward to live from your heart, all kinds of emotions may surface to make you aware of your belief systems, fears, and perception of yourself. This is an opportunity to allow the Spirit to unveil the truth and direct you to the next step. In order to fulfill your unique purpose on the earth, you will need to have your identity established on a solid foundation.

The writer of Colossians 3:3 tells us that *"your real life is hidden in Christ in God."* The Greek word for life in this passage is *zoé*, which expresses the highest and best form of life you are designed to live.

The NAS New Testament Greek Lexicon defines this "real life" as including "the absolute fullness of life... which belongs to God; life real and genuine."[47] What the passage in Colossians is saying is that your true identity, who you are at the core, can only be known in the context of your relationship with Jesus. As you get to know Jesus more, you will become aware of how you are made and how God sees you. As you choose to believe what He says about you and accept it as truth, you will establish your identity on a secure foundation. You will also become more fully alive and able to express your uniqueness when you learn to step forward in wholeness and freedom.

Created to Reflect His Image

Throughout your lifetime, you may have developed a belief about who you are based on other people's opinions and expectations. Or you may have based it on what you perceived was acceptable. You are meant to reflect God in such a way that when people see you, they know you belong to him.

As Erwin McManus writes, "The more your identity is rooted in what God says about you, then you will be less controlled by the opinion of others."[48] This is the kind of security God wants to establish in you. For purposes of understanding more about your true identity, here are five aspects of God's image that describe the real you!

1. God is relational. You are wired for connection and you aren't meant to do life alone. You are designed to interact and relate to God and to people around you. It doesn't matter whether you classify yourself as an introvert or an extrovert; you need people in your life if you're going to experience a healthy, more fulfilling life. Without meaningful connections with God and others, you will walk around on the earth feeling dead on the inside and without a clear vision.

2. God is creative. Part of the mandate of the first humans was to reproduce, create, and multiply. You and I are called to create with our words, hands, hearts, bodies, and souls. Creativity refers to the ability to express and develop ideas, love, beauty, and truth in unique ways. I believe every person has the capacity to create and demonstrate this powerful aspect of God's nature. It may simply be that you have been told otherwise, and limiting beliefs may be blocking your creative flow. Great ideas often get shut down because of lack of trust, misunderstanding, and misinterpreting what creativity is. Many entrepreneurs are mislabelled as scatter-brained and misunderstood because they have so many ideas and struggle with the ability to focus or follow through. You simply have to examine nature and the human body to see the creative work of God. You are wired to express this creativity in unique ways.

3. God is spiritual. You are primarily a spiritual being, having a temporary physical experience. God is Spirit and communicates with you through your spirit. You consist of a body, soul, and spirit, and you are a triune being like God. God's original intent was for your spirit to be the main operating system directing the actions of the soul and body. Living disconnected from God distorts the intended order and causes the soul to focus on human effort alone.

Jesus's death and resurrection restored your ability to become alive spiritually, with unhindered connection to the Spirit of God and to others. The power of godly love and true intimacy flows as a result of being filled with God's love and extends to others out of the overflow of a heart and soul that has been transformed. Jesus led the way by showing us how it is possible to be fully human yet fully alive spiritually while on the earth.

4. God is productive. You are designed to multiply, act, build, establish, and expand. The mandate given to Adam and Eve was to subdue the earth, multiply, and have dominion over everything. They were given the responsibility together, as man and woman, to rule the earth and to be productive in all they did. Work is therefore a godly concept and a reflection of the nature of God.

Like anything, however, work can take you off track if you look to it for your source of identity and security. Cycles of rest and productivity were modelled by God as part of who He is and how He made you and me to function on the earth. The challenge most people face is learning how to be productive while operating from a place of rest in God. Too often one is traded for the other, and when carried to the extreme this can lead to laziness or striving. We are not only created in God's image but also in his likeness, which means we are to operate the way He operates.

5. God is complete. You were created to live with a sense of fulfillment and completeness. Completeness means lacking nothing. Scripture confirms this fact:

> *By his divine power, God has given us everything we need for living a godly life. We have received all of this by coming to know him, the one who called us to himself by means of his marvelous glory and excellence.*
>
> —2 Peter 1:3

A beautiful painting is deemed valuable because of the artist, and the same is true with your life. You are valuable because you were made by the greatest Designer of all time, God Himself. Your value was further demonstrated by the cost God was willing to pay to restore spiritual connection with you. As you reconnect with the heart of God, uniting with Christ through the cross, you become complete, lacking nothing, and able to access everything you need to live the life you've been designed for.

Foundation of Trust

> *Trust in the Lord with all your heart; do not depend on your own understanding. Seek his will in all you do, and he will show you which path to take.*
>
> —Proverbs 3:5–6

Have you ever been betrayed? What was your immediate response? Probably anger, perhaps followed by a vow to never trust anyone again. This is a typical way of responding to hurt. After the shock or feeling of pain, the brain kicks into protection mode and suggests to you that it's probably a good idea to stop trusting people. The brain was designed to protect you as a first response.

That's what happened to me as a young teenager. When I first read Proverbs 3:5–6, the words jumped out at me. I experienced inner turmoil, giving God all the reasons I couldn't trust Him. Even though God wasn't the one who had hurt me in the past, I projected my pain onto Him. This is another typical response, especially when the person who broke your trust was a parent or someone in authority.

My experiences led me to search elsewhere to find security and feel safe. By age fourteen, my education had become my security and the most important thing in my life. If I didn't understand something, I didn't trust it. So when I came to know God, this was one of the first areas the Holy Spirit made me aware of. Proverbs 3:5–6 became the template for teaching me how to trust again.

Psychologists say that a person's ability to trust is established during the first five years of life, and if this foundation isn't laid the person will have difficulty developing close relationships. It may also lead to other behavioural difficulties and unhealthy patterns.

No family is perfect. No parent is perfect. That's why we need role models in order for us to learn how to love and relate from a pure heart. Through relational difficulties in our families, our ability to trust can grow or be shattered. For me, it was shattered. Growing up in a home filled with alcohol and domestic violence left me feeling confused, scared, and broken-hearted. Love became equal to pain. As a result, I decided that I wasn't going to trust anyone ever again.

This may be true for you and the reason why intimacy is such a scary concept to embrace. At one time, your heart was open, trusting certain people to care for it, but instead they wounded it. Your natural reaction was to close off your heart and numb the pain. That may work for a while, but sooner or later you'll discover that you can't have the very thing you desperately need, because you made heart-level decisions that are blocking you from accessing what you need.

Trust is a misunderstood concept. Trust is earned based on what you know to be true about the character of another person. Trust is a choice we make and a risk we take. It can be restored when damaged. It grows as we step out to believe in someone and they consistently come through. Trust is cultivated in an environment of love, humility, and faithfulness. Trust is foundational to human and spiritual connection. Trust is absolutely essential if you want to experience deeper levels of intimacy and wholeness. Trust is essential to stepping forward in true freedom.

As a young believer, when I came upon new and unfamiliar situations I struggled with trusting God for the unknown. To help me move forward, He challenged me with this: "If you can't trust Me for what you don't know, trust Me for what you *do* know. Trust Me for what you have experienced to be true of Me, where I have already been faithful to you. Let that be the basis for trusting Me as you move forward. As I met you before, I will meet you again."

This is my challenge to you. Step forward now and trust God for what you do know to be true of Him and let Him meet you in the unknown.

Foundation of Intimacy

Pastor Mike Bickle says,

To know Christ and be known by him means we experience intimacy at levels we previously never imagined could take place. He desires that all things hidden or private would be open before him. In return, he reveals the hidden things in his heart to us.[49]

In his book *Windows of the Soul*, author Ken Gire writes,

So much is distilled in our tears, not the least of which is wisdom in living life. From my own tears I learned that if you follow your tears, you will find your heart. And if you find your heart, you will find what is dear to God. And if you find what is dear to God, you will find the answer to how you should live your life.[50]

Many who seek God want the benefits of spiritual connection, such as salvation, healing, and blessing, but they don't understand that their deepest need is actually for intimacy. You may excuse it by saying, "I'm not that kind of person," "Only the really needy (weak) people need that," or "I'm not the sensitive type." As we discussed earlier, we are hardwired for intimacy. The problem is that you need to acknowledge your need for it before you can enjoy its amazing power. If intimacy scares you or seems out of reach, your resistance is most likely rooted in past hurts and distorted perceptions formed years earlier.

The late Jack Frost, author of *Experiencing the Father's Embrace*, says, "Love and intimacy are something we submit to before we can receive them."[51] I have found this to be so true in my life. When I chose to submit to God's love, and in doing so trust him, I discovered that I had room in my heart to receive His love and truth. The more I chose to engage my heart in the process, the more I experienced a closer intimacy with Him and the more I wanted to know Him. The simplest definition of intimacy is "to know and be known by someone."

As you embrace the process of transformation, you will be presented with opportunities to trust God in areas you never had to before and be invited to know more of his fullness. The starting point for experiencing intimacy in any relationship is to first acknowledge your need for intimacy and then be willing to engage in ongoing heart-level communication.

Bickle suggests that intimacy is cultivated in a relationship when these three behaviours are present.

1. Transparency. In the Garden of Eden, Adam and Eve are said to have been naked and unashamed. This is a picture of transparency wherein there is freedom for people to trust each other; there is no pretence or hidden agenda. In this model, the way you are in public is the same as the way you are in private. Who you are is clear and not confusing to others.

2. Connection in communication. Intimacy involves a two-way relationship in which you engage at the heart level, go beyond surface conversation, and experience a deeper understanding of another person.

3. Vulnerability. Vulnerability is the ability to admit your need for help at the risk of being rejected, hurt, and misunderstood. To experience intimacy and love, you have to be willing to risk getting hurt. Psalm 139 reminds us that even while we were being formed in our mothers' wombs, God was intimately acquainted with every part of us. His thoughts towards us were precious, and it He who knitted us to our mothers' wombs. When we were most vulnerable and helpless, God was near us, loving us. It is from this place of security in God's love that we can be free to be vulnerable with others as appropriate.

In Genesis 2:18, God said, *"It is not good for the man to be alone. I will make a helper who is just right for him."* By saying this, He implied that it's not good for us to have intimacy with Him alone. God's plan was for Adam to become aware of his need for connection beyond God and nature. After spending time with the animals, Adam realized that there was no one like him; he was becoming aware of his need for oneness and connection on a human level.

Jack Frost suggested that until Adam saw this, he could not be trusted with a woman.[52] Many men excuse themselves from engaging in heart-centred communication by saying that it's not who they are. However, Paul says in Ephesians 5:25–28 that men will not love and value themselves until they begin to love, cherish, and restore their wives through intimacy. By loving their wives intimately, they also demonstrate love for themselves, which by the way is an important requirement for being able to fulfill the Great Commandment:

"You must love the Lord your God with all your heart, all your soul, and all your mind." This is the first and greatest commandment. A second is equally important: "Love your neighbor as yourself." The entire law and all the demands of the prophets are based on these two commandments.

—Matthew 22:37–40

To summarize, transformation is an important process God uses to establish proper foundations in your life, foundations that are essential to fulfilling your unique purpose. As you come to know Him in all His fullness and embrace the truth, your beliefs will shift and change. You will experience new levels of freedom to live, just as Jesus did.

Does that mean you lose who you are? No, it's quite the opposite. The real you becomes freer to be expressed as you seek to live as Jesus lived and love as He loved. Like light shining through a diamond, your uniqueness will be seen as you allow His presence to flow through you unimpeded. This is the beauty of living in wholeness and holiness.

The famous author C.S. Lewis claimed that when you wholly belong to God, you are more yourself than ever before.[53] As you come to know Him more and more, your true self becomes unearthed, awakened, and more alive. His nature shines through your life in unique and life-giving ways. While living from that place, people will encounter Jesus as they interact with you.

Stepping Forward

- What is lacking in your foundation?
- What one step can you take today to demonstrate your trust in God to restore and establish the healthy foundations you need?
- Journal your discoveries.

Endnotes

46 There's nothing like the presence of God to expose the unhealthy areas in your heart.

47   "Zoe," *Bible Study Tools*. Date of access: June 25, 2018 (https://www.bible-studytools.com/lexicons/greek/nas/zoe.html).

48   McManus, *The Barbarian Way*, 70.

49   Bickle, *The Seven Longings of the Human Heart*, 100.

50   Ken Gire, *Windows of the Soul: Hearing God in the Everyday Moments of Your Life* (Grand Rapids, MI: Zondervan, 1996), 195.

51   Frost, *Experiencing the Father's Embrace*, 48.

52   Ibid., 44.

53   C.S. Lewis, *The Screwtape Letters* (New York, NY: MacMillan, 1961), 59.

chapter eight

Releasing the Real You

I am saying that we need to find the courage and freedom to be ourselves. We need to let ourselves become the unique individuals that God created us to be.[54]

—Erwin McManus

The second reason why it's important to embrace the process of transformation in your life is that it frees you walk out your divine purpose more fully. Instead of seeing your purpose as an event or end result, view it as a series of choices that unfold as you step forward with deliberateness, authenticity, and faith. With each step, you discover the uniqueness of who you are and how you are wired. As you keep on trusting that God is in the midst of the process, with each step forward you are being prepared and empowered to live in more freedom.

Many people want the end result and fail to value the process of getting there. In my experience, the process *is* the preparation you need to equip you for the next step in your adventure. It's also essential to complete this process in order to reach the desired outcome. For example, as a former long-distance runner in high school, I had to spend hours training each week to prepare for races. As I followed my coach's advice, embracing the process of training and discipline, I found myself better prepared to meet the challenges of the race and finish well.

> In my experience, the process IS the preparation you need to equip you for the next step in your adventure.

Beyond each new step in life is a place you have never walked before, including responsibilities and challenges that will require your faith and personal capacity to move beyond. What you learn in the process will prepare you to expand your capacity in three specific areas.

1. Knowing God. As you learned in a previous chapter, there are several dimensions to knowing God. When I was a new believer, an older couple in the church introduced me to the power of praying the Scriptures. One of the passages I started with was Ephesians 3:14–21, which became my personal prayer for a long time. In this passage, the apostle Paul discusses how the Spirit works to strengthen you with power deep in your core so that you can grasp all the dimensions of God's love. One purpose of embracing the process is to know this love that surpasses all knowledge so that you will be filled to the measure of all the fullness of God (Ephesians 3:19). This implies that the more you know God and experience His love, the more your capacity expands to be able to carry His heart into the situations you face in life.

John Eldredge, author of *Journey of Desire*, wrote,

This may come as a surprise to you: Christianity is not an invitation to become a moral person. It is not a program for getting into line or for reforming society. At its core, Christianity begins with an invitation to desire.[55]

The more you know God, the more you desire to know Him and become like Him. In the process, you will have opportunities to trust God for things you never had to trust Him for before. As you choose to trust Him, He reveals other aspects of His character and nature, moving your knowledge of Him from the head to the heart. Growth is a by-product of you discovering more about who God really is. This is affirmed in Colossians 1:10, which says that *"you will grow as you learn to know God better and better."* Experiential knowing replaces mental assent.

2. Growing in God. The J.B. Phillips translation of Colossians 1:29 says that we participate in the work of God *"so that, if possible, we may bring every [person] up to his full maturity in Christ"* (Phillips). This passage illustrates another goal of the process: to bring you to full maturity in your relationship with Christ. The process is described in both Galatians 4:19 and 2 Corinthians 3:19, respectively: *"until Christ is fully developed in your lives"* and *"as we are changed into his glorious likeness."* As you embrace the process of transformation, you will become more and more like your Heavenly Daddy. Eldredge reminds us, "Christianity has nothing to say to the person who is completely happy with the way things are. Its message is for those who hunger and thirst-for those who desire life as it was meant to be."[56]

Embracing the process involves expressing your desire and hunger for everything God made you to be. It requires a willingness to discover the depths of your heart, where passion and longing dwell, and having the courage to choose to live from that place while allowing your heart's capacity to be stretched and your mind renewed.

The Greek word for *grow* conveys the meaning that maturing spiritually involves an ongoing process. In 2 Peter 3:18, we are encouraged to *"grow in the grace and knowledge of our Lord and Savior Jesus Christ."* There is great power when someone possesses spiritual maturity in both of these areas: grace and knowledge. However, most people focus on one and neglect the other. Growing in God is not only meant to increase your knowledge and deepen your spiritual intimacy, but also to empower you to live from the heart He gave you.

Embracing the process is an essential key to developing spiritual maturity and being prepared for whatever lies ahead. The rewards of the process are best described in James 1:2–4:

> *Dear brothers and sisters, when troubles of any kind come your way, consider it an opportunity for great joy. For you know that when your faith is tested, your endurance has a chance to grow. So let it grow, for when your endurance is fully developed, you will be perfect and complete, needing nothing.*

3. Going for God. As you embrace the process of transformation, the Holy Spirit also expands your capacity to experience what I call the "full release." As you grow in your love for God, so does your desire to share this love with others you meet. As you cooperate with the work of the Holy Spirit in your life, you experience the freedom to move past your problems and focus on your purpose. One of your purposes is found in Matthew 28:18–20, where Jesus gave the Great Commission:

> *I have been given all authority in heaven and on earth. Therefore, go and make disciples of all the nations, baptizing them in the name of the Father and the Son and the Holy Spirit. Teach these new disciples to obey all the commands I have given you. And be sure of this: I am with you always, even to the end of the age.*

As you become freer to live the real you, you will want to share this new-found freedom with others. Your love for God will compel you to go to places you never previously imagined.

You were made to not only do the works Jesus did on the earth, but even greater works. This involves learning how to operate in your true authority and release His anointing more consistently. Freedom will flow from the intimacy you'll develop as you embrace His process of transformation.

Why a Process?

It has been argued that when Jesus said, "It is finished," He meant that there was no need for further healing, that a person is instantaneously whole the moment they become born again. However, what Jesus was actually referring to was the fact that He had completed the mission He'd come to the earth to carry out. He was part of a bigger plan that God the Father had set in motion to restore His people to an intimate relationship with Him. In order for that to happen, God had to do what mankind didn't have the power to do. This was the reason for Jesus's death and resurrection: to finish the work of removing the barrier that stood between us and God, therefore reconciling us.

In order for us to be fully restored into relationship with God, we also have a part to play. Our part involves accepting what Jesus did on the cross and receiving His gift of eternal life. In order to walk in our full capacity as sons and daughters of God, we need to be willing to engage the Spirit's work to restore us to wholeness.

Let us look at a passage in the book of Hebrews in order to understand this distinction between what's finished and what's not, and see why the transformation process is necessary: *"For by that one offering he forever made perfect those who are being made holy"* (Hebrews 10:14).

When you study the meaning of this verse in the original Greek, the distinction between the words "made perfect" and "being made holy" becomes much clearer. First of all, the verb tenses are different; "made perfect" is written in past tense and "being made holy" is written in continuous present tense. The Greek word for "perfect" used in this passage is derived from *teleios*, which means, "to complete, finish."[57] More specifically, it is *teleiomai*, which means, "to be made perfect or complete only in the sense of reaching one's prescribed goal."[58] When used elsewhere, *teleios* means, "not morally lacking"[59] (Romans 12:12, Colossians 3:14).

The word *teleios* is also used in Matthew 5:48, which says, *"But you are to be perfect, even as your Father in heaven is perfect."* Our western culture mindset interprets perfect to mean that a person never fails, never makes a mistake, and is flawless. The Oxford Dictionary defines it this way: "Having all the required or

desirable elements, qualities, or characteristics; as good as it is possible to be...
Absolute; complete."[60]

According to Strong's Concordance, *teleios* refers to fully completed growth—an adult, as contrasted with infancy and childhood; it can be used in a relative or absolute sense, such as God's perfection is absolute; and man's perfection is relative, and reaching the goal set for him with each individual differing according to his God-given ability. The *teleios* is one who has attained his moral end, the goal for which he was intended, his purpose, namely to a person obedient to Christ. When used in Matthew 5:48, the meaning is similar to "not morally lacking." In no way does the word mean "without sin."

So being made perfect means that Jesus completed the task of establishing man's moral standing with God. His death fulfilled the requirements of the law. He completed the work He was sent to the earth to do. He took the consequences for our wrongdoing so that we could be free to live and have access to everything we need in order to live as we were created to. By this one act, all the barriers were removed. This was the task that Jesus said was finished. It was accomplished. His purpose was fulfilled. From a legal standpoint, we have all been declared innocent, and therefore perfect, or justified, to stand before God.

To further illustrate this point, pretend that you were convicted of a crime and the bail was set at one million dollars. If you didn't have the money, you would have to go to jail. But suppose someone came along who loves you and pays your bail so you can go free. Legally, you can stand before the court as a free man or woman. All you have to do is accept the gift of a paid ransom and walk out of jail. That's what Jesus did on the cross; He paid the ransom for you to go free. The difference is that He paid the ransom with His life. When God looks at you, He sees you as innocent and worthy to be in relationship with Him. God's part is finished. All that's left for you to do is receive the gift, reconnect with God, and respond in faith and obedience.

The second part of Hebrews 10:14 refers to *"those who are being made holy."* Here, the verb tense implies an ongoing process of being sanctified or made whole. The Greek word used for "being made holy" is the verb *hagiazo*, which comes from the word *hagios*, which means separation, set apart, consecration, devotion to God, sharing in God's purity, and abstaining from earth's defilement. Thus, *hagiazo*, as used in this passage, means "to purify internally by renewing of the soul, set apart for God, to be, as it were, exclusively his."[61] More specifically, it means "to separate from profane things and dedicate oneself to God."[62] This is the process of choosing every day to live your life aligned to God's standard of truth, connecting with Him as your source, and cooperating with the activity of the Holy Spirit in your life for the purpose of restoring you to your original purpose.

To better understand this concept, consider the following analogy. When I received my master's degree in speech-language therapy, I was a full-fledged speech-language pathologist (SLP). I had a certificate that declared my expertise and qualified me to apply for jobs in that field. However, I still had to go out and put into practice all my expertise in helping people overcome speech and language difficulties. I had all the tools, knowledge, and credentials I needed. That part was finished. All that was left was to apply what I knew, to believe that I was indeed an SLP, even when I made mistakes or had to consult with other SLPs. This was my part.

As you begin to implement the truth, you will face challenges that require you to go back, remind yourself of what you need to do, and learn to apply what you know to be true. After one mistake, you could tell yourself, "I'm not really a (insert specialty here), since I made that mistake." I'm sure you would agree this is silly—just like it would be silly to say to a toddler learning to walk that he will never be able to walk because he's fallen down too many times.

Change and growth are an ongoing part of life. When you enter a marriage relationship, you become one with your spouse, and every day you learn how to walk out that reality. You both come from different backgrounds and mindsets, so even though you may be *one* spiritually, you will experience differences and difficulties along the adventure of life. As you engage at the heart level with your spouse, submitting to each other, you get to know each other better and fall more deeply in love. You grow in understanding and learn to walk out life together. So it is with learning to walk in unity with God and in your identity as His son or daughter. This adventure of learning how to live out who you really are involves getting to know God better and trusting Him as your source of truth, life, and love.

Although the cross was messy, it was the starting point of your restoration. In fact, the heart of humanity was so scarred and wounded from the effects of being disconnected from its source that God created a new heart—to help us start over in rebuilding our lives while enjoying an adventure of love and intimacy with Him. God did His part. It was finished on the cross. As you choose to spiritually connect with God and stay connected, you will discover who you really are. Through the process you will learn how to receive and give love from a whole heart and relate to others from a place of truth, love, and authenticity.

In summary, the transformation process involves a partnership between you and the Holy Spirit. The full process involves you responding to the Holy Spirit's invitation to step forward in faith and obedience. Exactly what your part looks like is the discussion we'll tackle in the next section of this book.

Stepping Forward

- What process is God inviting you to participate in at this time in your life?
- What one action can you take this week to embrace that process?
- Journal your discoveries.

Endnotes

54 McManus, *The Barbarian Way*, 133.

55 Eldredge, *Journey of Desire*, 36.

56 Ibid., 36.

57 James Strong, *Strong's Exhaustive Concordance*. Date of access: June 27, 2018 (https://www.biblestudytools.com/concordances/strongs-exhaustive-con-cordance), #G5046.

58 Ibid., #G5048.

59 Ibid., #G5047.

60 "Perfect," *Oxford Living Dictionaries: English*. Date of access: June 25, 2018 (https://en.oxforddictionaries.com/definition/perfect).

61 James Strong, *Strong's Exhaustive Concordance*. Date of access: June 27, 2018 (https://www.biblestudytools.com/concordances/strongs-exhaustive-con-cordance), #G37.

62 Ibid.

chapter nine

Reflecting His Glory

For God, who said, "Let there be light in the darkness," has made this light shine in our hearts so we could know the glory of God that is seen in the face of Jesus Christ.
—2 Corinthians 4:6

Did the travelling circus ever come to your town? If so, do you remember visiting a booth called the House of Mirrors? When I was a child, I remember looking into these mirrors and marvelling at how different they made me look. Each mirror distorted my body in some way, never giving an accurate reflection of what I really looked like. If I had believed the distorted reflections, it would have driven me to make drastic changes to myself. Those distorted perception were, in essence, lies.

That's exactly how I felt when I struggled with anorexia. My heart and mind were etched with distorted images of how my body looked. Believing those images to be truth almost killed me! Your perceptions become your reality. If your perceptions are distorted, they can lead you into deception and perpetuate destructive patterns in your life.

Another reason that it's so important to embrace God's process is that through it you can glorify God by how you live. This involves allowing the Holy Spirit to expose any distorted perceptions and being willing to have your reality transformed. Embracing the process isn't always easy, comfortable, or neatly ordered, but it's the path to greater joy, intimacy, and freedom. How you show up in the process determines the success of the future.

I grew up on the east coast of Canada, along the Atlantic Ocean. I remember many incidents when local fishermen were caught at sea due to unexpected storms and couldn't see their way home. The lighthouse was their only hope. When the brilliance of that light shines, it overshadows and hides the structure in which it is contained. It doesn't matter if the tower is old, cracked, or otherwise in need of repair; as long as the light is unobstructed and shines brightly, it guides fishermen home to safety.

The same God who spoke into the darkness and created light made the light of His presence shine in your heart so you could know His glory (2 Corinthians 4:6). As you open your heart to connect and get to know Jesus, the light of His presence fills your soul and overflows with love to others. This light is very powerful because it is the very essence of God. Jesus was described as having the *"fullness of God a human body"* (Colossians 2:9), and when you connect with Him this fullness resides in you, too. Just as with a lighthouse, the light in your spirit is meant to shine through you to impact the world.

The following passage likens us to clay pots with a treasure inside: *"We now have this light shining in our hearts, but we ourselves are like fragile clay jars containing this great treasure. This makes it clear that our great power is from God, not from ourselves"* (2 Corinthians 4:7).

Think of a clay pot. If there's a light inside, how will others see it? There are only two ways for the light to escape: through an opening in the top of the jar or through any cracks in the jar. For God's light to shine through us, reaching people in our world, it shines through the cracks. What are these cracks? They are the imperfections, the scars of past hurts, the brokenness, frailties, and those experiences of life you normally want to hide from others. 2 Corinthians 4:7 reveals that it's through these imperfections that God's glory is released to others.

How can you let His light shine through the cracks? The light shines through when you are honest about your past, your struggles, where you've come from, and what you're walking through, and when you give Him credit for carrying you through it all. As you allow His Spirit to meet you in those wounded areas, to heal and deliver you, you can access His power and presence to step forward. It is in your areas of greatest vulnerability and weakness that God is most glorified. As you look to Him for strength and grace, He empowers you to do what you couldn't do on your own, and He

Instead of hiding weaknesses, focus on being hidden in Christ.

frees you to live the real you. This draws attention to Him, highlighting Him as the source of your freedom. It inspires people and gives them a desire to know Him better as they see Him empowering you.

Instead of hiding weaknesses, focus on being hidden in Christ. Focus on giving Him the glory for giving you what you need to complete the transformation process.

The Good Kind of Suffering

Have you ever prayed something like this: "Show me your glory, Lord" or "Be glorified in my life, Jesus"? Do you realize what you're praying for? I certainly didn't the first few times I prayed that way. It seemed like a glamorous thing to have His glory shine through my life, like winning the Oscars or some other reward. Oh, it's a reward for sure, but not because of all the great things we've done. It's only a reward because of His mercy and grace.

If you want to reflect His nature or glory, you have to be willing to also participate in His sufferings (Romans 8:17). In fact, the Bible says that it's actually a privilege for you to share in His sufferings (Philippians 1:29). I'm not saying you are to seek suffering for the sake of suffering. My point is that you're not to fear trials and sufferings but instead learn to embrace the process of what God can do in you through them. A passage in the book of James says it well:

> When all kinds of trials and temptations crowd into your lives my brothers, don't resent them as intruders, but welcome them as friends! Realise that they come to test your faith and to produce in you the quality of endurance. But let the process go on until that endurance is fully developed, and you will find you have become men of mature character with the right sort of independence. And if, in the process, any of you does not know how to meet any particular problem he has only to ask God—who gives generously to all men without making them feel foolish or guilty—and he may be quite sure that the necessary wisdom will be given him.
>
> —James 1:2–6, Phillips

The Message translation puts it this way:

> Consider it a sheer gift, friends, when tests and challenges come at you from all sides. You know that under pressure, your faith-life is forced into the open and

shows its true colors. So don't try to get out of anything prematurely. Let it do its work so you become mature and well-developed, not deficient in any way.
—James 1:2–4, MSG

The good kind of suffering produces good fruit in your life, such as making you *"not deficient in any way."* Jesus brought glory to His Father by the way He lived, what He said, and what He did, which included suffering. We are called to do the same. However, don't try to bring on suffering by actively sinning and disregarding God's instructions. This kind of suffering produces very different results and you want to avoid them at all costs. Don't suffer for suffering's sake. But when you're walking in harmony with God and suffering happens, take the apostle James's advice and *"let it do its work so you become mature and well-developed."* This good kind of suffering is part of the transformation process that leads to freedom and wholeness.

The Deep Work of God

Suffering is uncomfortable, no matter what. Why does a good and loving God allow pain and suffering in the world? This has been a topic of much debate throughout the centuries. The commonly held belief seems to be that all suffering is evil and that sin is the only cause of suffering. Therefore, if you're suffering you need to get rid of it as soon as possible.

Many Christians still walk in this mindset today, and often unknowingly. It can lead Christians to feel shame and fear about what others would think of them if they were to admit their struggles in life. It hinders the process and prevents many from living authentically. Viewing suffering in this way can stunt a person's growth and maturity in Christ. The process of becoming transformed into His likeness can become that much more difficult as we resist what God is doing.

Laurie Beth Jones said in her book, *Jesus Life Coach*, "God's will does not take the path of least resistance. Remember, the path of least resistance is often downhill."[63] Don't settle for the easy route. Embracing change and the process of transformation can be uncomfortable and challenging, yet it's the path that will lead you to the life you dream of, filled with spiritual adventure, intimacy, and increased fulfillment.

Jesus told us to expect trials and trouble and to not lose heart because of them, but instead access the same power to overcome them as He did (John

16:33). As you draw upon His resources, you will gain what you need to grow through every trial that comes your way.

You don't have to look far to discover that many of God's closest friends experienced troubles and suffering. A few examples from the Old Testament include King David (1–2 Samuel), Joseph (Genesis 37, 39), and even the great prophet Elijah (1 Kings 19). Even Jesus's closest friends experienced times of emotional and spiritual distress. One of the most famous accounts is when Peter denied ever knowing Jesus and then plunged into deep despair. John the Baptist, who had been chosen to prepare the way for Jesus, was imprisoned and eventually beheaded. Even the most dedicated missionary, the Apostle Paul, endured tremendous life-threatening trials. The classical spiritual writer Jean Pierre de Caussade once said, "God instructs the heart, not through ideas but through suffering and adversity."[64]

Is it possible that God accomplishes His deepest, most profound work in us not in times of peace and comfort but in the times of our greatest turmoil? Author of *Seasons of the Soul* Bruce Demarest has observed that "disorienting experiences highlight how fragile we humans are and how desperately we need to grow strong in the Lord."[65] It is through these difficult seasons of our life that God gets our attention, awakens our soul to our need for Him, and, according to Demartest, "points out a better path to maturity and fruitfulness."[66] He goes on to describe the need for young Christians to yield, like a young colt that needs to be broken and trained: "God lovingly breaks us in order to retrain and reform us. While we experience God's presence, these situations of crisis and emptiness both test and stress our relationship with God."[67] Some refer to this as a crisis of faith, or identity. Like a broken arm that didn't set properly, a doctor may need to rebreak it so that it can heal properly.

Beauty and Pain

Mike Bickle writes in his book *The Seven Longings of The Human Heart*,

> The two most powerful realities that move the human heart are beauty and pain. While we will be forever exhilarated with the beauty of Jesus, some of our greatest times of intimacy with Him will be fellowship in the midst of suffering as we endure pain and hardship…
>
> The pain of persecution and the pain of our failure actually serve as escorts to know and experience Jesus at more intimate levels. When

our hearts are hurting and starving to be comforted, He will be most vivid in our experience if we allow Him.[68]

1 Peter 5: 10 says, *"So after you have suffered a little while, he will restore you, support, and strengthen you…"* The processes of God are designed to restore you to abiding peace, lasting joy, and deeper intimacy, with the ultimate goal of having Christ be more fully formed within you.

An unexpected disappointment, sudden illness, or significant turn of events can leave even the most mature Christian stunned, emotionally shaken, and weakened. The psalmist speaks of such an experience in Psalm 143:4: *"I am losing all hope; I am paralyzed with fear."*

Theologian A.W. Tozer says,

To do his Supreme work of grace within you he will take from your heart everything you love most. Everything you trust in will go from you. Piles of ashes will lie where your most precious treasures used to be.[69]

Perhaps you have discovered what I have, that God sometimes offends your mind to expose your heart. This is part of His process of renewing your mind so that it doesn't block your heart from fully expressing His.

You see, God is after your heart. He is completely devoted to you and asks the same from you. His love burns for greater connection with you, and it's in your darkest moments that you will experience the sweetest expressions of His love—if you are open to receive. Our sorrow and pain can either make us reach for a numbing agent or make us more alive to the present moment and the movements of His Spirit within us.

The life cycle of a butterfly is a fitting reminder that dark and painful times can produce the greatest work of maturing us and shaping our character. Demarest describes this cycle and reminds us that

the butterfly beats its wings against the walls of its cocoon in order to break free from its encasement. If someone were to assist the butterfly's escape by forcing a hole in its cocoon, the butterfly would not have gained the strength necessary to survive, and so it would die.[70]

While dialoguing with my husband David in the early stages of our premarital relationship, I described aspects of the healing process I had experienced in previous years. This is what I wrote in an email to him:

> I spoke of cocooning earlier. It is the most amazing experience (of course looking back from the other side—not fun in the moment). Here you are, hidden away, separated from people in spirit, emotion and space, held in a dark place unable to move and break through, hearing nothing and feeling nothing from anyone-except the pain and agony of internal growth and change, a stretching and deepening of every fibre of your being. You know there are people out there, but they are not yours to touch or care for in that moment. Every breath is consumed with drawing nourishment and strength from the source of your very existence, just to keep living, and feeding the expansion that's happening in your soul. In the midst of utter darkness, there are bursts of unspeakable joy and hope, as the Light brushes over you like the stroking of a paintbrush. It is a strange thing how both darkness and joy can coexist. It reminds me of the passage in Isaiah 45:3: "And I will give you treasures hidden in the darkness—secret riches. I will do this so you may know that I am the Lord, the God of Israel, the One who calls you by name."

You see, just because we don't understand what God is doing in any given moment doesn't mean He isn't at work in our lives. Just as John speaks of pruning a vine for greater fruitfulness, and Isaiah speaks of the refining fire, we are told of the potential for suffering and trials to refine our soul and shape our character. Indeed, Jesus, who was without sin, learned obedience through the things He suffered. Why should we think we can escape such processes?

One type of suffering is a healthy part of walking with God. Author Howard Hendricks states that problems we face are "God's chisel to shape the soul. He tests us to develop us, and he urges us to not give up or perform an abortion on His divine purposes."[71] Hendricks goes on to say that although we all want to become like Christ, we often "shun the process."[72]

When life is going well, we tend to rely on our own strength and resources. It's when life starts to get uncomfortable that we often seek help outside ourselves. However, for some people, life has to get *really* bad before they turn to

God. Demarest put it succinctly when he said, "We pursue God when the pain of remaining unchanged is greater than the effort needed to change and grow."[73]

Even though several passages in Scripture warn us to expect trials and tribulations as a normal part of life, we often seem shocked when we encounter them. I want to challenge you to consider that some suffering may actually be God's answer to your prayers to have Christ fully formed in you.

Demarest believes that "seasons of distress can deepen our relationship with God."[74] Hendricks said, "Suffering is God's melting pot to shape the soul. And none of us is exempt from the process. God's curriculum is not an elective; it is a required course designed to make us like His Son, Jesus Christ."[75] C.S. Lewis went so far as to label trials and suffering the "severe mercy" of God.[76] His love is pure and His process is safe to trust.

Treasures Formed in Darkness

Many years ago, someone prophesied over me that God saw me as a diamond. Several years later, I received a similar word. At the time, I didn't feel like a diamond, but that didn't change the fact that God's original intent for my life was to be like a diamond and reflect His glory. Diamonds are multifaceted and create brilliant colours as light is reflected through their sides from different angles. Diamonds are beautiful and valuable, but they are also formed under extreme pressure. Just like a caterpillar may not feel like a butterfly, only when it embraces the process does its true identity and purpose become a reality.

When trials and difficulties come, don't let them rob you of the truth of who you are and your unique purpose. You may experience times of intense darkness and extreme discomfort, but choose to believe that God is still at work.

Over the years, God has brought me through a series of processes to unearth, clean, polish, and bring me closer to Him. As mentioned above, during one of the processes God revealed what He was doing by directing me to read Isaiah 45:3, which talks about the treasures that can be formed in dark places. I came to understand how precious dark times are to God. That which may look like a dry, barren, depressing season to you may be the place where God extracts the finest gold. Demarest points out, "In His wisdom, God often turns up the heat when he sees gold worth purifying."[77]

No matter what the circumstances of your life may be, believing the truth about who you are is essential to living the real you and allowing God's glory to be revealed through you. I believe more than anything that He wants to release His glory from within His people to be seen and heard, to be expressed and expanded.

You have such a huge capacity within you that you don't realize. Your potential isn't about what you can do, it's about who you really are because of what He has already done for you. It's not about your ability but His ability flowing through you. You are meant to carry His heart to the people around you and reflect His very nature. This is why embracing the process is so key. In the next few chapters, we'll discuss how to posture your soul through this process.

Stepping Forward

- What is your perception of God? Do you believe He is good?
- How do you respond to trials and suffering in your life?
- What trial has God used to draw you closer to Him?
- What trial are you facing today that may be an opportunity for you to grow in God?
- For your further study, here are ten of the many rewards you will receive when you choose to embrace the process:
  - You will learn obedience (Hebrews 5:8, Psalm 119: 71).
  - You will share in His glory (Romans 8:17).
  - You will become equipped to help others (Hebrews 10:32).
  - You will experience greater intimacy with God (Hebrews 4:15, Philippians 1:29).
  - You will have increased spiritual maturity (James 1:4).
  - You will have the life of Jesus reflected in your life (2 Corinthians 4:10).
  - You will be refined (Isaiah 48:10).
  - You will be able to distinguish good from evil (Hebrews 5:14).
  - You will have increased authority (Luke 9:1).
  - You will become a partner with Christ (1 Peter 4:13).
- Journal your discoveries.

Endnotes

63   Laurie Beth Jones, *Jesus Life Coach* (Nashville, TN: Nelson Business, 2004), 196.

64 Bruce Demarest, *Seasons of the Soul: Stages of Spiritual Development* (Downers Grove, IL: Intervarsity Press, 2009), 51.

65 Ibid., 43.

66 Ibid.

67 Ibid.

68 Bickle, *The Seven Longings of the Human Heart*, 103.

69 A.W. Tozer, *The Incredible Christian* (Beaverlodge, AB: Horizon House, 1977), 122.

70 Demarest, *Seasons of the Soul*, 53.

71 Hendricks, *Color Outside the Lines*, 93.

72 Ibid.

73 Demarest, *Seasons of the Soul*, 53.

74 Ibid.

75 Hendricks, *Color Outside the Lines*, 9.

76 Sheldon Vanauken, *Severe Mercy* (San Francisco, CA: Harper & Row, 1977), 209–210. Quoting C.S. Lewis.

77 Demarest, *Seasons of the Soul*, 55.

Key #3
ALIGNMENT

———————————

The more your identity is rooted in God's value for you, the less you are controlled and limited by what others think of you.[78]

——Erwin McManus

chapter ten

What's Your Part?

What I go through does not define who I am. How I go through it defines who I am.[79]

—Valorie Burton

I'm probably more passionate than most about the importance of embracing God's process because of my own journey and the thousands of people I've coached over the years. Countless individuals feel stuck emotionally and don't know how to step forward and experience true freedom. They have never been taught how to embrace the process of transformation and resolve the painful experiences that may be holding them back.

One young Korean lady I knew was so used to stuffing down her pain that even when she wanted to cry, she couldn't. When she first came to see me, her dark, vacant eyes screamed of pain and numbness.

Her story is not uncommon. After years of being put down by her mom, the message she came to believe in her heart was that she was worthless and didn't deserve to live. She had stopped crying years earlier from her parents mocking her. They'd told her that crying was a sign of weakness and that she should never have been born.

As a result of adopting these beliefs, she hardened her heart and became cold and disconnected, unable to let anyone close enough to really know her. Years later, she couldn't engage her heart in conversation, even when she desperately wanted to. This led to frustration and loneliness. She felt like she didn't belong anywhere or with anyone and couldn't trust that God loved her.

Perhaps you have a similar story. Perhaps you've gone through life minimizing the impact of an experience, trying to deny or bury the emotions or beliefs that surrounded it, and ended up not really knowing yourself and unable to

Lisa Vanderkwaak

connect with God or those closest to you. You may feel stuck because you were never allowed to express the emotions that emerged as a child. You were never taught how to deal with disappointment, betrayal, rejection, loss, anger, or other painful emotions, so as a child you did whatever you could to cope with the hurt. This often leads a person to unconsciously make decisions about what they need to do to survive and manage the resulting behaviour patterns.

By embracing the process today, you are giving God permission to go beneath the surface of your life to reveal distorted beliefs, heal your wounds, align your thinking to His truth, and set you free to receive His love in deeper levels of your heart.

God is love and will not violate your will. Therefore, the transformation process involves a partnership between you and the Holy Spirit. God initiated the process by doing what you were unable to do. He then offered you a whole new heart that's alive and equipped with the capacity to make the right choices and develop intimate relationships.

Your part is simply to respond. Part of this response involves making a deliberate choice to take God at His word and then align your thoughts and actions to reflect this choice. How you respond will determine the thoroughness of the process and whether you will experience the full measure of the freedom that comes as you learn to live from this new heart.

Understanding Your Part in the Process

In 2003, my family moved from Vancouver, British Columbia to Edmonton, Alberta in response to God's call. I wasn't prepared for the culture shock I experienced after moving to Edmonton. In small ways, I related to what Abraham must have felt when God called him to leave everything that was familiar, including family, house, and friends, and go to a place he didn't know. I could also relate to how people of other cultures must feel when they leave their homelands and go to live in a foreign country.

After leaving behind family, friends, and ministry partners, not to mention years of memories in a city I had known like the back of my hand, here I was in an unfamiliar place with people I didn't know.

In addition to having to adjust to differences in climate, landscape, job, and regional mentality, I found myself extremely disoriented and unable to get my geographical bearings. I'm a person who normally adapts easily to new

92

surroundings, so these feelings caught me off-guard. In Vancouver, the mountain range was to the north, a natural marker to help point me in the right direction. In Edmonton, the landscape is flat and wide open, with no familiar indicators of which direction you're driving. My internal GPS needed to be recalibrated to my new environment. Needless to say, I wasted a lot of time going in circles before familiarizing myself with my new surroundings.

When you make a decision to connect spiritually with God and live from your "new heart," you need to make some adjustments in order to successfully navigate your new way of living. You may feel inadequate, confused, or even disorientated.

To help you know what adjustments to make and align your internal compass, the Holy Spirit is always available to teach you everything you need to know, every step of the way. All you need to do is be open to learn and be actively engaged in the process.

Once you accept the invitation to enter into a relationship with God and spiritually connect with Him, your heart and spirit become awakened to the voice of His Spirit inside you. That's when the ongoing process of transformation begins and the Holy Spirit is activated to begin the work of bringing you deeper in intimacy with the Father. It's a lifestyle of aligning your body, soul, and spirit with the realities of heaven (Colossians 3:3).

As was discussed earlier, this ongoing process of being made holy is commonly referred to as sanctification and involves the active participation of both you and the Holy Spirit to bring it to full completion. Before discussing in more detail what exactly your role involves, let's briefly look at how the Holy Spirit works.

Let's review 2 Corinthians 3:16–18:

But whenever someone turns to the Lord, the veil is taken away. For the Lord is the Spirit, and wherever the Spirit of the Lord is, there is freedom. So all of us who have had that veil removed can see and reflect the glory of the Lord. And the Lord—who is the Spirit—makes us more and more like him as we are changed into his glorious image.

This passage states that as the Holy Spirit works in our lives, we become more like Christ and reflect His glory even more. Other parts of Scripture reveal the exact work of the Holy Spirit and how He does it. Here is a list of some of the ways He may communicate with you to bring you closer in intimacy with Him.

- He counsels you (John 14:17).
- He leads you into truth (John 15:26, 16:13).
- He lives in you (John 14:17–20).
- He reveals Jesus to you (John 14:21).
- He teaches you everything (John 14:26).
- He reminds you things God said (John 14:26).
- He brings you peace of mind and heart (John 14:27).
- He convicts you of sin and righteousness (John 16:7).
- He reveals future events (John 16:13).
- He glorifies Father God and Jesus (John 15:8, 16:14).
- He shapes you into the character of Christ (2 Corinthians 3:18).
- He leads you into freedom (2 Corinthians 3:17).

The three primary ways through which the Holy Spirit communicates with you are the scripture, the voice of the Spirit within you, and everyday life interactions, or any combination of these three.

The important thing to remember about the process is that your job is not to go digging for areas to work on. Let the Holy Spirit bring to your attention what shifts need to happen when the time is right. As He does, your job will be to respond with a humble, obedient heart. As you become aware of what's blocking you at the heart level, you will become responsible to do something about it. What you do next will become clearer as you continue to dialogue with Him and trust Him throughout the process.

Often people get stuck in a process not because of the obstacles they face, but rather because of their response to those obstacles. As you start to connect in meaningful ways with others, you may discover some areas of resistance within your heart. You may also become aware of unhealthy behaviours or distorted perceptions that may be keeping you from living the real you and embracing life fully. Conflicts, trials, transition, and loss serve to heighten this awareness and bring us face to face with the reality of our inner world.

> **Often people get stuck in a process not because of the obstacles they face, but rather because of their response to those obstacles.**

Exposing the motives or wounds of your heart may leave you feeling vulnerable and tempt you to run and hide, to avoid feeling the pain. In one of her TED

Talks, well known sociologist Brené Brown reported research findings showing that when people try to numb their emotional pain with substances, such as medication, those substances cannot isolate which emotion to numb so all emotions get affected.

In moments of vulnerability, if you choose instead to listen to your heart, face the pain, and yield to the work of the Holy Spirit to bring you comfort and healing, you will experience greater freedom and lasting peace.

Types of Responses

Transformation happens at the heart level and touches every part of your being. Scripture states that your soul can prosper, which in turn can lead to health in all areas of your life. The book of ancient Proverbs commands us, *"Guard your heart above all else, for it determines the course of your life."* Living the real you will involve not only accepting the invitation to align your human spirit to God's Spirit, but also a willingness to align your mind, will, and emotions.

Your willpower is one of the most powerful tools you possess, but willpower alone doesn't bring lasting transformation. It was given to you as a gift from God, who wants you to be able to choose from your heart. Having the freedom to choose is a sign of true love. You may struggle with making decisions in fear of making a mistake or being judged. Perhaps somewhere in your life you gave up your will to someone else's control. In the process, it's essential that you take back your will to choose and learn to exercise it in healthy ways. Choose to respond in obedience to the Holy Spirit and step forward in faith as He directs. Your ability to choose is a critical step in creating your future and experiencing wholeness and lasting freedom.

Your exact role in the process involves three main categories of responses: cooperation, consecration, and calibration. Woven throughout all three are the threads of confession and change.

In the coming chapter, we'll take a more specific look at each of these categories of responses.

Stepping Forward

- In what areas do you feel stuck and unable to move forward?
- What do you believe will happen if you step forward in that area? What will happen if you don't?

- If you struggle with making decisions, pray this prayer:

> Forgive me, Lord, if at any point in my life I gave up my will to choose and relinquished it to someone else. Today I take back my will and release all fears to You. I submit my will to You and You alone and trust You to guide and direct me in the way I should go. Teach me how to exercise my authority to make healthy choices as I purpose to walk in obedience to You. Thank You for Your wisdom and for restoring my soul.

- Journal your discoveries.

Endnotes

78 Erwin McManus, *Unleashed: Release the Untamed Faith Within* (Nashville, TN: Thomas Nelson, 2011), 70.

79 Valorie Burton, *Where Will You Go from Here?* 151.

chapter eleven

Cooperation

Sadly, we are often our own worst enemies when we take into our beings the very ideas and beliefs that hurt us far more than help us.[80]

—Dr. Don Colbert

As a young girl, I loved music but never had the opportunity to take music lessons or own an instrument. That was until I was twelve years old and my mom surprised me with a piano organ for my birthday. I was very excited and began to teach myself how to play. A short time after that, my parents separated, and as a result me, my mom, and two of my brothers moved to another city. Although we couldn't take the piano organ with us, my mom said that we would come back for it as soon as we could.

A year later, my parents got back together and we moved back home. I was looking forward to resuming my music lessons. However, when I arrived home I couldn't find my piano organ anywhere. It was gone. When I asked my dad about it, my heart sank at his response: "I sold it. You left it behind, so I didn't think you wanted it."

All my dreams of learning how to play the piano were dashed.

Many years later, the Holy Spirit reminded me of this incident and revealed what had actually taken place in my heart that day. As I sought to understand my dad's decision to sell my piano, the conclusion I'd come to as a young girl was that the desires of my heart weren't important. This message got written on my heart that day as personal truth. Regardless of my dad's reasons, this was my perception.

Our perceptions become our truth and form part of our core beliefs. If left unchallenged, distorted perceptions lead to deception. I had formed a belief that the desires of my heart weren't important, and this led me to make an unconscious decision to disconnect myself from those desires. As a result, I began to devalue what was really important to me and ignore my true self. Even though I loved music and wanted to learn an instrument and take dance lessons, I didn't pursue it anymore. This was the beginning of a whole set of decisions that led me down a path of self-sufficiency, anorexia, and the quest to be perfect.

> If left unchallenged, distorted perceptions lead to deception.

What you believe to be true determines how you approach and respond to life. Your choices are very powerful, even if unconsciously made. Proverbs 23:7 says, *"For as he thinks in his heart, so is he"* (NKJV). To repeat what I said before: what you perceive to be true becomes your reality. What you believe to be true about yourself, God, life, and love will show up in your actions.

Your heart may have secret beliefs that your conscious mind isn't aware of until God reveals it to you. This is what happened to me that day. I had been denying part of how I was wired, ignoring the desires of my heart. It was too painful to believe for something for myself that other people didn't value and that might eventually be taken away.

During my first year of graduate school, several years after becoming a Christian, God decided that it was time to remind me of this event. It came in the form of a prophetic word from a stranger who didn't know anything about me. He was a Christian minister, speaking at a university campus meeting, and after he finished speaking he prayed for me and told me words that God was telling him to share with me. He told me things that only God could know, desires that had been locked away deep in my heart. He affirmed to me how God had wired me and who the real me was.

I left that meeting with a firm belief that God did love me and that He had given me those desires—and that He had given me permission to embrace them. God challenged my perception and brought the real truth to me.

That day, I made a decision to cooperate with whatever the Spirit was doing in my heart.

Amazingly, the years that followed were strategic in terms of my spiritual development. I began to experience deeper healing and the freedom to dream again. Interestingly, the area that I had been hurt in—my desire to express myself through music—was one of the areas God used to bring about the deepest healing in my soul. Through it, I learned to engage my heart in prayer and worship.

Getting to the Root of the Matter

God desires to rewrite the messages on your heart. In order to do that, He will both point out the bad fruit in your life and uncover the root of where those behaviours stem from. In order for a tree to be healthy, it must have a healthy root system. If the fruit on a tree is diseased, rotten, or stunted in its growth, removing the fruit won't solve the problem. The same is true in your life. When you become aware of a bad attitude, destructive habit, or unhealthy pattern of relating to others, you need to allow God to show you the root of where it all began.

A few years after this first campus meeting, I became part of a ministry team that held women's conferences throughout the region. One year, Linda Pender, a Christian counsellor from Kirkland, Washington, was the keynote speaker at one of the conferences. In a session, she spoke about the importance of getting to the root of presenting issues in your life. To illustrate, she drew a simple diagram, which I have adapted on the following page.

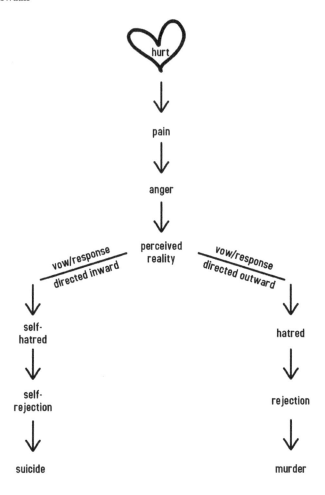

This diagram helps to explain exactly what can happen when you get hurt. Emotionally speaking, you feel pain and a normal response to pain is fear or anger. Depending on your personality and how you process pain, your anger will show up in different ways.

The moment of choice comes either when you first feel the pain, or when the response of anger occurs. What will you do with those feelings?

In the diagram, the path on the right shows what happens when unresolved pain is outwardly expressed. The unresolved anger can lead you to hate the person who hurt you, then reject them, and eventually it could lead to murder. The path on the left side of the diagram shows the progression if you mostly turn your anger inward. You hate yourself for being treated that way, reject yourself, and potentially end up taking your own life.

The root was the initial hurt, and the way in which you respond to it determines its long-term effect on you. Remember, you can't change the past, but you can change your responses to the past. You are only defined by your past to the degree that you want to be. Where is your present life held back because of past hurts?

When you have limiting beliefs, you keep running up against limits in your life—because you always get what you believe. The heart protects as truth whatever you decide is normal. The scriptures give us tools for transformation, but most people don't experience lasting transformation because they don't know how to use these tools. Furthermore, most people don't allow change to penetrate the depths of their hearts. Instead they settle for behaviour modification and wonder why they still feel stuck and unable to move forward.

Understanding Pain

Feeling emotional pain is sometimes a gift in that it indicates that you're alive and that you haven't completely shut down your heart. In my experience, running from hurt only serves to intensify the pain and darkness at a later date. You may find yourself crying out to God during your most intense times of suffering, saying, "I can't take anymore." When the pain of staying the same becomes greater than the pain of changing, that's when you'll finally acknowledge your need for help.

You're right in believing that you won't be able to take too much more on your own. But if you learn to access God as your ultimate source, you'll feel empowered to overcome whatever stands in your way. As you choose to embrace His process, your capacity will expand and you will find yourself getting stronger and able to endure more. This is what's often referred to as being "stretched."

Procrastination is often tolerated as an acceptable behaviour, but in reality it's an indication that we are more motivated by pain; we don't make a change until we feel the threat of the painful consequences of not completing the task. Pain can be a powerful motivator and serve to alert us when something needs attention. However, love is an even more powerful motivator and creates more lasting change. If pain is our only motivator, then once the pain is gone we often go back to what was.

Engaging in the process involves learning to obey God from a place of intimate love for Him and trusting Him above all others. This kind of response produces deep transformation. Learn to embrace change as your friend and face pain when it happens. This is an opportunity to access the resources of heaven, freeing you up to step forward and fulfill your purpose.

Wholehearted Living

Freedom begins when you choose to exchange reactions for healthy responses. Co-operating with the Holy Spirit means allowing Him to show you what took place in your heart at the moment you experienced the painful emotion. As He reminds you of the hurtful experience, ask Him to show you what message was written on your heart in the past. In other words, what did you perceive to be true and how did you decide to deal with that truth? What did you do with the pain you felt? How did you decide to cope with your perceived reality so you could survive?

Once I understood what had happened in my heart regarding the piano incident, I cooperated with the Holy Spirit by doing five things.

First, I *repented* for believing a lie and for bitterly judging my dad for not caring for me and for selling my piano. Then I *renounced* the lie that my desires weren't important. Renouncing something means no longer agreeing with it. By doing so, you take away the power of that lie to control your actions.

Thirdly, I *released* the pain and hurt from my soul and laid them at the cross, and in exchange I *received* the healing, comfort, and truth in my heart that was made available to me through the resurrection of Jesus and the Word.

Finally, I changed my *response* by choosing to bless instead of curse, and to forgive the person who had hurt me. Most importantly, I chose to believe the Word for what was true and to determine my reality.

Jesus Led the Way

Isaiah 53:5 says that Jesus *"was pierced for our rebellion, crushed for our sins. He was beaten so we could be whole. He was whipped so we could be healed."* He is the only one capable of carrying the pain we feel. He was already crushed by the weight so we don't have to be anymore.

Your part in the transformation process is to surrender your will and cooperate with the Holy Spirit as He works in your life to reveal truth and make you free to love and receive love. God wants to awaken your heart to what is true, expand your capacity to flow in his fullness, and set you free to live the real you. The enemy of your soul tries to deceive you to believe that there is something wrong with you and make you feel condemned for going through times of testing and trials. That's because he knows that you carry the very presence of God inside you. He wants to stop you from fully radiating His glory through your life.

Jesus came to the earth as a human to show us how to navigate through the trials and tests that come our way. In fact, we are told that the Holy Spirit was the one who led Jesus into the place of testing (Mathew 4:1). He allowed Jesus to undergo testing from the enemy. God didn't do the testing or the tempting but He allowed the enemy to do it, knowing that it was necessary for Jesus, as a human, to walk in the strength, character, and fullness of God to fulfill His purpose.

In fact, Jesus understands what it means and feels like to embrace the process. Hebrews 4:15–16 says,

> This High Priest of ours understands our weaknesses, for he faced all of the same testings we do, yet he did not sin. So let us come boldly to the throne of our gracious God. There we will receive his mercy, and we will find grace to help us when we need it most.

Jesus modelled the way to embrace the process. During times of struggle, He willingly cooperated with the work of the Holy Spirit and stayed connected. He went to a quiet place to pray and converse with God. He surrendered His will to do the will of His Father. He drew strength, courage, wisdom, and power from His source of life to focus and fulfill His purpose. As He embraced unconditional love and allowed that love to be deeply rooted in his soul, it established the foundations of identity, trust, and intimacy needed to complete His assignment on the earth.

You can take comfort in knowing that Jesus knows and is intimately acquainted with the process. While on the earth He lived as a human, and as such He endured every kind of testing known to mankind. He willingly embraced the process by cooperating with the Spirit, knowing it was producing in Him what was needed for what lay ahead.

Although Jesus faced temptations, He didn't give in to them. Instead He submitted to God and accessed the power to overcome sin. This is the life we are created to live.

Stepping Forward

- How can you learn from Jesus's example about how to respond in the process?
- Here's a simple prayer for you to use whenever you need to deal with unresolved pain and experience freedom to move forward.

Lord, I give You my pain and release it from my soul. I also release all defilement and painful memories that were deposited into my soul and apply the blood of Jesus to wash away all their residue. Thank You, Jesus, for dying on the cross both to deal with my sin and to carry my pain and sorrow. I receive Your healing and bind Your peace and comfort to my soul. I declare healing and wholeness in the deepest parts of me and thank You for setting me free to walk in Your ways.

• Journal your discoveries.

Endnotes

80   Colbert, *Deadly Emotions*, 152.

chapter twelve

Consecration

When we turn to God, His love transforms us and ignites a new passion within us.[81]

—Erwin McManus

Several years ago, I was at a conference in Guatemala and met a woman who was the personal intercessor for a well-known prophet in the United States. We found ourselves on the same bus tour one day, travelling to see the famous city of Almolonga, which had previously experienced community transformation.

Being new to prayer, I wanted to glean from her experience and wisdom, so I asked, "What would you say is the most important key to more effective intercession?"

Without hesitating, she looked at me with her warm, strong eyes. "Stay clean, stay close, and stay connected."

Her words vibrated in my soul and still do to this day.

When Joshua was given the responsibility of leading the children of Israel into the Promised Land, God instructed him to tell the people, *"Purify yourselves, for tomorrow the Lord will do great wonders among you"* (Joshua 3:5). The word used here for purify means to consecrate, to sanctify, or to set apart. It refers to aligning the motives of your heart to God's heart, so they are consistent with the new nature you have been given.

Purification also involves cutting away anything that isn't in alignment with who you are and the life you were created for. This is a painful yet sometimes necessary part of the process. Luke 6:43–45 describes it this way:

A good tree can't produce bad fruit, and a bad tree can't produce good fruit. A tree is identified by its fruit. Figs are never gathered from thornbushes, and grapes are not picked from bramble bushes. A good person produces good things from the treasury of a good heart, and an evil person produces evil things from the treasury of an evil heart. What you say flows from what is in your heart.

Just like a tree won't produce good fruit unless its roots are healthy and strong, the Holy Spirit may first highlight some of the bad fruit in your life in order to get to the root. This includes the obvious areas of your life, such as habits or patterns of behaving. But even though it may be obvious to other people, you may be blind to it.

However, the Holy Spirit doesn't just want you to change your behaviour; He wants to free your heart so you can choose to live according to your new nature. He does this by inviting you to believe His truth and allowing Him to reveal and heal the wounded areas of your soul.

In addition to uprooting things in your heart that are destructive and unhealthy, the Holy Spirit also works to cultivate even more fruit from the areas that are already healthy and productive. John 15:2 describes it this way: *"He cuts off every branch of mine that doesn't produce fruit, and he prunes the branches that do bear fruit so they will produce even more."* This is a powerful principle to remember when stepping forward. The goodness of God aims to free us to walk in His fullness and have a transformational impact on others.

If you're becoming aware of bad fruit in your life, such as unhealthy patterns, addictions, negative attitudes, and unforgiveness, then it would serve you well to ask God to show you the root. In other words, ask Him to expose the unresolved pain or wounds in your heart and the subsequent belief system that formed to feed that behaviour. To promote further healing, it's important to understand the specific nature of your wound.

There are three main types of actions that can cause a person to be wounded.

1. Sins you commit and their consequences. These are actions you are responsible for, such as choices you made that resulted in hurting yourself or others.

2. Sins of omission. This refers to areas of unmet needs in the early years of your life when significant people neglected to give you what you needed, resulting in unstable foundations being formed in your heart. These include the good things like affection, security, trust, healthy love, provision, shelter, and protection. If unresolved, this type of wound can lead to problems in relationships where you look to others to fulfill your unmet needs, and you never feel satisfied. The truth is that only God can fully satisfy this deep hole and meet those core needs.

3. Sins of commission. These are the unjust things that others did to you. These hurts can create fear in you and cause you to be stuck, unable to move forward emotionally. These painful experiences need to be processed in order to understand how you interpreted what happened to you and how your heart responded.

How to Process Painful Experiences

For the first type of wound listed above, the healing may be as simple as repenting for the unwise choices you have made and wrong things you have done. However, sometimes there are consequences that you'll have to walk through in the natural even after repentance. For the other two types of wounds, the resulting issues must be resolved or they will continue to affect your relationships.

Most believers understand that God wants to free them from their past so that they won't be held back. The common response is to overlook pain, minimize it, and stay focused on the present. This approach, however, will lead to serious denial and produce all kinds of bad fruit in your life. Hebrews 12:15 warns us, *"Look after each other so that none of you fails to receive the grace of God. Watch out that no poisonous root of bitterness grows up to trouble you, corrupting many."* Simply putting a Band-Aid on a cut that needs to be cleaned will result in an infection. Emotionally, your wounds need the same care, otherwise you may find yourself reacting to people and situations in a manner that is inappropriate and illogical.

Your reaction is triggered by something that you perceive to be a similar experience to the original painful moment. These types of reactions indicate that you may have unresolved issues, and that your past is negatively impacting your present.

In her book, *Successful Women Think Differently*, Valorie Burton writes that "reactions are what you feel, say and do as a result of your thoughts… [and] every reaction you have is a result of a thought."[82] That's why it is so important to address what you believe in your heart to be true. As you saw from the diagram in the last chapter, changing how you perceive life will often result in changes in your responses.

The natural human reaction to getting hurt is to feel pain, whether it's physical or emotional. And when you feel pain, the next natural reaction will either be fear or anger. Both are normal, healthy responses to feeling rejected, judged, or misunderstood. It's what you do with the initial emotion that may lead to sin or cause you to get stuck emotionally. As illustrated previously, your pain will be manifested either inwardly or outwardly, depending on how you process your emotions. If you don't attend to the area of hurt soon after it occurs, your normal responses can turn to unhealthy reactions and lead to more destructive behaviours. This is what the Bible refers to as infected wounds in Isaiah 1:6: *"You are battered from head to foot—covered with bruises, welts, and infected wounds—without any soothing ointments or bandages."*

In my experience, a wound can become infected in two ways.

1. Reacting in unhealthy ways. You can react in unhealthy ways and make inner vows or unconscious decisions about how you'll cope with the pain. This was what happened to me when my parents divorced and my dad refused to pay child support. Since no one sat me down to explain what was happening, I was left to conclude on my own that my dad didn't love me and I wasn't worthy to be supported. The truth, however, is that my dad was angry towards my mom for divorcing him and was trying to get revenge by not providing for us. It wasn't until years later that I realized he had simply been acting out of his own pain.

As a result of what I perceived to be true, these messages became imprinted on my heart: "No one will take care of me" and "My dad doesn't love me." I further decided that in order to deal with the pain of this reality—remember, whatever you perceive to be true becomes your reality—I couldn't trust anyone to be there for me, so I had to take care of myself. I decided that I didn't need anyone. These inner vows led me down a track of destructive behaviours that left me alone and emotionally bankrupt, hurting even more than ever. It was my reaction to the event that kept me stuck, not the event itself.

When you react to pain instead of resolving it, two things can happen to keep you stuck in that pain. The first is what my counsellor friend Linda describes as having a message written on your heart. These are perceptions that you formulated based on your interpretation of the painful event. They are also referred to as limiting beliefs which you adopt as truth. They lead you to make internal decisions about how you'll cope with your perceived reality. These decisions become very binding, limiting you to a specific way of living or responding to life as a means of survival. They become your default mode.

Here are some examples of common vows people make:

- "I will never be like my mom/dad."
- "I will never let anyone hurt me again."
- "I will never share my heart again with anyone."
- "I will not trust anyone."
- "I will always reject them before they reject me."
- "I will never depend on anyone except myself."

These decisions are like binding agreements. They have tremendous power over your body, emotions, and spirit and are usually the result of some bitter judgment you've made towards someone out of pain and anger. They can be unconscious decisions made in your heart and mind. They are often referred to as inner vows. You believe that these inner determinations are protecting you, but in fact they act like prison walls, surrounding your heart and preventing the flow of love in and out. Some inner vows may seem good, but they need to be renounced and broken, because they restrict your spirit's freedom to cooperate with God and to receive all that you need to move forward. What may have served you well at one time, helping you survive, now blocks you from living the real you as God created

2. You allow normal emotions to control you. Another way in which a wound gets infected is when you let normal emotional reactions control you. Anger is one such normal reaction.

Ephesians 4:26 warns us, *"'[D]on't sin by letting anger gain control over you.' Don't let the sun go down while you are still angry."* This verse reveals that anger becomes sinful when we hang on to it and let it gain control over us.

There are five ways in which anger can gain control over you: when you hang on to it and allow it to turn to bitterness (Hebrews 12:15), judgments (Matthew 7:1–2), unforgiveness (Matthew 18:35), hatred and rage (1 John 2:9), and demonic influence (Ephesians 4:27).

The power to effect change in your own life is in your own hands, and it's exercised in how you respond to what life throws your way. By embracing the process of properly resolving the wounds of the past, your healing will be so thorough and complete that all remains will be a painless scar. You may not forget the experience, but you'll be free to move forward in wholeness and maturity.

> **Embracing transformation is embracing life itself, no matter how painful it may be.**

Embracing transformation is embracing life itself, no matter how painful it may be. This involves consecrating yourself to God and allowing Him to purify and cleanse your heart from the residue of sin and painful experiences. It means making a choice not to let anger gain control over you and instead stay close to God so He can give you what you need in order to deal with the hurt.

The Power of Your Choice

As you engage your heart and embrace the process of growth, you essentially cultivate trust and intimacy. In order to allow God to complete the work of transformation in your life, it will require a series of choices on your part. These include choosing the following.

Give God permission to change you at the heart level. It's important to understand that attending to the condition of your heart is essential to stepping forward. Jesus's mission on the earth is outlined in Luke 4:18–9 and includes healing broken hearts and bringing freedom to your soul so that you can live the real you. He is interested in your heart! As you allow healing to take place, your heart's capacity to love will expand and you will find yourself being an inspiration and catalyst for healing in the people around you. God won't force His way into your heart; you must invite Him to heal so that you can experience the increased freedom to step forward and fulfill your unique purpose.

Name your emotions. This may seem strange to say, but many Christ-followers don't allow God to move in their emotions, and as a result they remain stuck for years. Many view emotions as part of their sin nature and try to suppress them. As you tune in to your heart and identify the wounded areas of your soul, strong emotions may surface and painful memories may be evoked. Tears may start to flow, so let them flow! God gave you tears for a reason, one of which is to make you aware of what's really going on in your heart, and to help you live wholeheartedly. Ignoring the signs will only serve to disconnect you from your heart and deny reality. As you acknowledge where you have felt hurt, for example, and put a name to the emotion, allow the pain to surface and the wound to be cleansed.

In my years of experience working with individuals in the area of personal and spiritual growth, I have found this to be an absolutely essential step in the process of transformation. Grieving a wound is important to the process of becoming whole and experience true freedom. Don't minimize the impact of the wound and try to be strong and not show emotion. Among other things, denying emotions only serves to disconnect you and impede the flow of love in and out of your heart.

When the light on your car's dashboard lets you know that your gas tank is low, you pay attention. Similarly, when your emotions are stirred, it indicates that something is being touched at the heart level and needs your attention.

The messages written on your heart are tied to the emotions you've felt at critical times in your life, and transformation only happens when truth affects change in your heart. Equally important as acknowledging the pain is choosing not to stay in your brokenness. By intentionally releasing the pain to God, you make room for Him to give you comfort and healing in exchange.

Resist the temptation to share all of your wounded emotions with anyone who will listen. Intentionally seek out trusted individuals who are spiritually mature and able to help you move past the pain to a place of healing and wholeness.

Choose to receive God's love. This is where the bonds of intimacy and trust become stronger. In your most vulnerable moments, allow His perfect love to penetrate your heart and dispel all fear. Being able to receive is very difficult for many people and can hinder their growth in God. This was true for me, and at different points along my journey of growing in intimacy with God I had to learn to intentionally receive. The first was when I was fifteen and had to admit that I needed forgiveness. Then again, at various times as I grew in my relationship with God, He invited me to deliberately lay aside pride and self-sufficiency and open my heart to receive what I needed. Every time I made this choice, I experienced another level of freedom.

Here's an example of a prayer that enables you to receive what God is offering:

Lord, I need You. I give You the pain of feeling rejected by (name the person) and invite you to heal the wound in my heart. I open my heart to You and receive Your comfort, healing, and love. Thank You, Lord. Amen.

While grieving my loss, one of the ways the Holy Spirit ministered to me was through a song called "Held" by Natalie Grant. The song reminded me that God never said that everything would always go the way I expected, and when it doesn't I can be assured that He will always be there waiting to hold me—if I allow Him to. As I listened to the words of the song, I felt waves of love flood my soul and bring me healing and comfort.

Release those who have hurt you. I have discovered that many people don't understand what forgiveness really is. First and foremost, forgiveness is a choice, an act of one's will. It's not a feeling. If you wait until you feel like forgiving someone, it may never happen. Secondly, forgiveness is a gift and not something that can be earned. Trust, on the other hand, does need to be earned. Therefore, forgiving someone doesn't mean you have to trust them again.

When I first became aware of my need to forgive my father, I prayed like this: "Lord, I forgive my dad for what he did to me. Help me to feel that forgiveness and to live it." I was just a new believer and I didn't understand anything about forgiveness, but I prayed the way that I sensed the Holy Spirit leading me. I prayed that prayer every day for many months, until my forgiveness sank in at the heart level. I acted in faith, behaved like I had forgiven him, and within a few months the feelings of forgiveness accompanied my actions.

Today, I understand a lot more about forgiveness and have discovered that unless forgiveness reaches the point where it affects the emotions connected to the hurt, it will not be complete. This is affirmed in Matthew 18:35, where Jesus ended a parable with these words: *"That's what my heavenly Father will do to you if you refuse to forgive your brothers and sisters from your heart."*

One way you'll know that you have truly forgiven from the heart is when you feel compassion towards your offender. You will then be able to see them in the way God sees them, and not experience the sting of the previous pain.

A young woman I once met had the stereotypical type A personality. Outwardly, she looked put-together: well groomed, not a hair out of place, focused, and intense. She was driven to achieve and produced results that blew her colleagues out of the water. Inwardly, she was tormented by feelings of insecurity, fatigue, and constant anxiety. When asked questions related to her inner world, she would quickly change the topic to avoid going there.

She had struggled for years living a double life—one that others saw, and another one that no one saw except God. The day she exercised courage and chose to let God reconnect her to her own heart, she began to really live. For years she had avoided engaging her heart, because she had stuffed down so many painful memories and didn't want to face them. However, she discovered that day that the first step is the hardest! Once she acknowledged to God that she was stuck and needed His help, it unlocked her emotions and released her pain. He then empowered her to extend forgiveness and walk in freedom.

Stepping Forward

- What choices do you need to make today to help you get emotionally unstuck?
- What emotions do you need to pay attention to and give a name to?
- What first step can you take today to move you forward in the process?
- Journal your discoveries.

Endnotes

81   McManus, *The Barbarian Way*, 101.

82   Valorie Burton, *Successful Women Think Differently* (Eugene, OR: Harvest House, 2012), 136.

chapter thirteen

Calibration

The question is, are you willing to synchronize your timing with the divine timing?[83]

—Valorie Burton

A few years ago, I developed pain in my lower back and went to see a chiropractor for the first time in my life. After a thorough assessment, Dr. Jason gently touched my spine and made small but deliberate adjustments. Amazingly, it not only cleared up the pain but it gave me more energy.

As I continued to receive treatments, I thought about how many physical illnesses can be triggered by your spine being out of alignment, even slightly. The chiropractor's job is make sure your spine is properly aligned so that your body can function as it was originally designed. Similarly, in order to live the life you were designed for, your spirit, soul, and body may need to undergo some adjustments.

You were put on this earth for a reason. Stepping forward is all about aligning your heart and actions so that you can function more fully in wholeness and lasting freedom.

At this point, I need to warn you that aligning your heart to His heart will wreck life as it is for you at the moment. You may start to feel uncomfortable and overwhelmed as you experience the love He has for people! You may be challenged when He asks you do something that's out of the box or beyond your comfort zone. However, if you still choose to bring your heart into alignment with His, life will take on a whole new meaning, bringing tremendous joy, deeper fulfillment, and abiding peace.

What exactly does it mean to align your heart? To better understand this concept, I like to use the analogy of calibrating an instrument. According to the online *Merriam-Webster Dictionary*, the act of calibrating means to standardize (something, as a measuring instrument) by determining the deviation from a standard so as to ascertain the proper correction factors... to adjust precisely for a particular function...[84]

When you tune an instrument, you align it to a standard frequency. When you calibrate your heart to God's, you're measuring it up against His nature and seeing where your nature needs to be adjusted so that it matches the way in which He loves and responds.

Just like an instrument can get out of tune, your heart can lose calibration and require frequent check-ins to. Colossians 3:1 says that we should *"set [our] sights on the realities of heaven."* This involves a willingness on your part to let the Holy Spirit examine your thoughts, intentions, motives, and actions to bring about the necessary adjustments and fine-tuning.

God's heart is so big, compassionate, and generous that I cannot possibly carry his Heart on my own strength and ability. So my constant prayer is that He will expand my capacity to contain the fullness of His love and presence, so that I can have a greater impact on the people around me. My job is to make room in my heart.

James's Four-Step Process

After you become aware of where your heart may be out of tune, of where it may have deviated from God's standard of love, you'll need to intentionally calibrate it to get back into alignment. The book of James outlines a four-step process of calibrating your life to function the way God designed you to function.

1. Accept the truth. This first involves facing the truth of the condition of your spiritual relationship, and then accepting God's truth as your standard for living. James 1:21 says, *"[H]umbly accept the word God has planted in your hearts, for it has the power to save your souls."* The word translated here as "save" is the Greek word *sozo*, which means to heal and make whole.[85]

2. Act on the truth. Your actions show what you really believe. James 2:14 speaks bluntly about this: *"What good is it, dear brothers and sisters, if you say you have faith but don't show it by your actions? Can that kind of faith save anyone?"* In fact, James says that it is your actions that make your faith complete (James 2:22). The Holy Spirit will reveal truth to you and it's up to you to apply it to your life. After you humbly accept the truth, James adds that you need to act on it: *"But* *don't just listen to God's word. You must do what it says. Otherwise, you are only fooling yourselves"* (James 1:22).

3. Adjust as you go. You've probably heard the saying that says it's easier to steer a moving vehicle than to push one that's stationary. This is also true for your life. It's better to keep moving forward, even in small steps, than to keep stopping and starting over. Most people give up when they make a mistake instead of simply making course corrections and continuing on.

Learn to value progress over perfection. Adjusting as you go is a key element to living the real you and walking in freedom and wholeness. When you do this, you will see life as an adventure rather than a race to get from A to B. James compared it to looking at yourself in the mirror and ignoring the fact that your hair is messy, your face is dirty, and you need to get more sleep. Adjusting as you go requires you to take responsibility for what you can do at any given moment and inviting the Holy Spirit to complete the deeper work of deliverance, healing, and transformation.

> *For if you listen to the word and don't obey, it is like glancing at your face in a mirror. You see yourself, walk away, and forget what you look like.*
>
> —James 1:23–24

4. Actively engage. Lastly, calibrating your heart to function as you are designed to will require a commitment to keep actively engaging with the Holy Spirit as your ultimate source of life. By doing so, you take personal responsibility for your growth and don't just let life happen. As you seek to deepen your spiritual relationship, you participate more fully as a partner in the process and enjoy a richer, more fulfilling experience. James said that you will be blessed: *"But if you look carefully into the perfect law that sets you free, and if you do what it says and don't forget what you heard, then God will bless you for doing it"* (James 1:25).

Ongoing calibration promotes a life of wholeness and integrity that others will be drawn to. It also makes you ready in season and out, prepared for every good work at a moment's notice. It empowers you to experience deeper levels of intimacy and unity with others, as well as true freedom. You will become a likely candidate when God is looking for a heart that's devoted to His.

The scriptures talk about the benefits of having a heart that is calibrated:

Blessed are the pure in heart, for they will see God.

—Matthew 5:8, NIV

The eyes of the Lord search the whole earth in order to strengthen those whose hearts are fully committed to him.

—2 Chronicles 16:9

Expect Shifts

When you commit to keeping your heart aligned to God's heart, you will experience ongoing shifts in the following ways.

You'll have a clean conscience. You'll find yourself not settling for the smallest violations of your conscience. You will have a growing desire for purity in the deepest levels of your heart, which will lead you to be quicker to repent when you say a careless word or do something that may hurt you or others. You may also find yourself no longer settling for ways of living that you once tolerated in the fear of being rejected or singled out for your beliefs—tolerations which can be viewed as blatant compromises to your faith. Becoming pure in heart relates to having your heart aligned to God's heart and operating from the perspective of His love and truth. As a result, your conscience will become more tender and alive.

You will experience greater intimacy with God. As you commit to keeping your heart regularly calibrated, you will experience closer intimacy with Him and be awakened to His presence in everyday life. You will find yourself seeing what He sees and aligning your actions to join in on what He's already doing. This is how Jesus lived. He only did what He saw the Father doing. Your desire for closeness and intimacy will increase and grow.

You will feel more connected to God. This is different than closeness in that it relates to a sense of belonging. You will begin to feel like you are valuable, part of a family and plan much bigger than imagined. You will experience a growing awareness that you are in the right place and have a part to play in fulfilling the purposes of God on the earth. This connectedness will become stronger as you purpose in your heart to stay closely aligned to His heart and realize that who you are impacts others around you. You have been created to walk in unity and interconnectedness with others in your community of faith. Proverbs 4:13 encourages us, *"Take hold of my instructions; don't let them go. Guard them, for they are the key to life."*

You will be centred. When I was in my twenties, I started taking ballet and Pilates classes. I had always loved dance but never had the opportunity as a child to take formal lessons. One of the disciplines I learned was how to find my "centre." Being in tune with my centre helped strengthen my core muscles. This was essential in learning to maintain stability and strength in my movements and posture. Learning to lean into my centre especially helped me stand strong and steady when uneven surfaces threatened to throw me off balance or knock me down. Having a strong centre helped my movements become more focused and accurate.

In everyday life, it's equally important that you learn to get in touch with your centre, your heart, and strengthen the core of who you really are and the values you hold. Discovering the real you and embracing your true identity will enable you to make the necessary adjustments along the way as you continue to step forward. Being able to connect and stay centred to your heart will provide you the ability to get back on track when life seems out of control. It will keep you standing strong and resilient.

The same is true in decision-making. As you identify who you are at the core and what is true, you will have more clarity around choices and experience less stress when faced with potentially overwhelming circumstances.

Finding your centre is all about alignment and embracing the real you. According to the dictionary, aligning something involves the process of adjusting its component parts so that they are in proper relative position.[86] Aligning your actions is about making the necessary changes to how you do life so that it expresses who the real you is and reflects the realities of heaven.

Change is seldom easy, but it can be accomplished if you make the commitment to change small and change often. The daily calibration process will become automatic and more fine-tuned as you seek to know God more in the following three areas.

1. His Word. The first way to understand who you are is in understanding what God's Word says about you and aligning your heart to live by His truth. I will warn you that you may not always *feel* like it's truth, and if you let your feelings alone be your guide you may never experience the joy of living who you really are. You must believe that God's Word is the absolute truth and that all other truth is secondary to it. In fact, Jesus proclaimed to *be* the truth, personified. Believing His Word and acting on it will lead you to a life of extreme freedom and joy, no matter your circumstances.

While I was studying at the University of Ottawa, I was introduced to an older couple, Terri and Glen, who were passionately in love with God. Whenever I heard them speak, I felt a hunger inside me to know God more. I am forever thankful for this couple for imparting a love of the Word into my life and for teaching me the power of praying the Scriptures in a personal way.

The discipline of praying Scripture significantly impacted my life. Making the Word of God personal and applying it to your life starts with believing it as your truth, and making it your plumb line of truth. Using Ephesians 1:17–18 as my example, I would pray like this:

> God, I ask You, the glorious Father of our Lord Jesus Christ, to give me spiritual wisdom and insight so that I might grow in my knowledge of You. I pray that my heart will be flooded with light so that I can understand the confident hope You have given to me, as Your called and holy one who is part of Your rich and glorious inheritance.

As you engage with God in this way through His Word, you will discover where your beliefs need to be adjusted before you are able step forward in wholeness and freedom.

2. His will. Living as a human, Jesus recognized the need to constantly check in to make sure that what His heart desired was not just His own human will, but aligned to the will of His Father. This is a great example for us to follow, because sometimes our desires can be so strong and noble, so seemingly good, that they can get us off track—that is, if our will isn't surrendered to His. That's why it is important to cultivate relationships with others so that we share mutual trust and love, giving them permission to speak into our lives to remind us of what's true.

3. His ways. It's one thing to know God, but it's another thing to know His ways. The Scriptures tell us that His ways are not our ways. This has everything to do with His character, which is consistent and unchanging. As you come to know His ways, you will be able to discern what you need to do in any given situation.

One thing is for sure: God's way is always better and more thorough than ours, even though we may not understand it all the time.

True Reflection

You have a vital part to play in this process of becoming like Christ. Not only are you encouraged to look into the mirror of God's Word to see yourself, but as you make that spiritual connection your life can become like a mirror that brightly reflects who He is.

In the second letter to the Corinthian church, the Holy Spirit is put front and centre (2 Corinthians 3:17–18). It says that wherever the Holy Spirit is, you will experience freedom. This isn't about the freedom to do whatever you want without consequences, but rather the freedom to choose to do what it is right. When you live disconnected from God, your heart and spirit are bent on doing your own thing, and you aren't free to choose to do the right things.

Transformation is not a one-time event, but rather a process to embrace, initiated by the Holy Spirit, to make us more like Christ and to free us to live our real selves. The J.B. Phillips translation of 2 Corinthians 3:18 says it like this: *"But all of us who are Christians have no veils on our faces, but reflect like mirrors the glory of the Lord"* (Phillips, emphasis added).

As I studied this verse more, and specifically the word "mirrors," I came across some Bible commentary that shed some light on the concept:

> It was the property of mirrors back in those days (which were made of a flat, circular piece of cast metal) that the more polished the surface, the clearer the image. Continuous elbow grease was needed to keep away corrosion.[87]

The is a provocative picture. The life and ministry of the believer are depicted as a mirror in need of continual cleansing so as to reflect to an ever-increasing extent the glorious knowledge of Father God.

The decisions you make today will affect your tomorrow and what your future will look like. The glory of God will cover the face of the earth when His children learn to walk in wholeness and freedom. As you calibrate your heart, make ongoing adjustments to your lifestyle, and take responsibility for your part in the process of transformation, your life will take on more clarity, meaning, and influence. Remember, making small changes consistently over an extended period of time is far more effective than making huge changes sporadically. Let the Holy Spirit lead you through the steps.

Stepping Forward

- How can you start to take responsibility for your part in the transformation process?
- Where in your life do you need to follow the four-step process outlined in the book of James?

- In what areas are you already experiencing one of the shifts discussed above?
- What is coming up in your heart and mind as you reflect on these shifts?
- Journal your discoveries.

Endnotes

83   Valorie Burton, *Following Your Unique Path to Extraordinary Success* (Colorado Springs, CO: Waterbrook Press, 2004), 163.

84   "Calibrate," *Merriam-Webster.* Date of access: June 26, 2018 (https://www.merriam-webster.com/dictionary/calibrate).

85   James Strong, *Strong's Exhaustive Concordance.* Date of access: June 27, 2018 (https://www.biblestudytools.com/concordances/strongs-exhaustive-concordance), #G4982.

86   "Alignment," *Dictionary.com.* Date of access: June 26, 2018 (http://www.dictionary.com/browse/alignment).

87   Linda L. Belleville, *2 Corinthians: The IVP New Testament Commentary Series* (Downers Grove, IL: Intervarsity Press, 1996), 112.

chapter fourteen

The Power of Clean Vision

He wants to use your experience to deepen your ability to love and serve the people He brings into your life.[88]

—Valorie Burton

Have you ever watched a 3D movie without wearing 3D glasses? It's not very enjoyable, is it? With the proper glasses, you can see a clear picture. One time, my kids had a pair of glasses that had an image of an animal right in the centre of the lens. Every time they looked through the glasses, they saw the animal on everything. They had other glasses with pink-coloured lenses; when they wore those glasses, everything looked pink.

The truth is that everyone views life through coloured glasses. The problem is that we don't realize it. The coloured glasses represent our life experiences, personal biases, limited knowledge, wounded hearts, and unresolved issues. My friend Shannell said it this way on a Facebook post one day: "When you look through the world with a broken lens, the world looks shattered." Your perception determines your reality.

I first became aware of my own coloured glasses when I was at university. While attending church, I found myself resisting the head pastor's words. Even though I liked him as a person, my heart kept doubting his sincerity. As I asked God to show me what was going on, He revealed to me that I was looking at this pastor through the lens of my experience with my father. When I was growing up, my father had been unpredictable and unsafe to be around. This experience left me with a distorted perception of authority figures, and therefore my belief about my father became generalized to include all people in authority, even God. I had concluded in my heart that people in authority could not be trusted—and now I was projecting this perception onto my pastor. When I realized this, I went to my pastor and asked him to forgive me for wrongly judging him in my heart. That broke the resistance and opened the door for me to walk in greater freedom under his spiritual leadership.

Part of the work of the Spirit is to wash away anything that interferes with us being able to live wholeheartedly and fully alive in body, soul, and spirit. Along the journey of letting the real you live more fully, you will become clearer about who you are and your unique purpose on the earth. You will have many opportunities to give in to the expectations of others and abandon your dreams. Having clarity about where you're going and what's possible will empower you to keep moving forward when confusion and overwhelm try to lead you off-course.

One of my speaking mentors, Craig Valentine, has a saying about this: "A clear mind says go, and a confused mind says no." When your vision and thinking is clear, you can move forward with confidence.

Having clarity about who you are and who God is in you empowers you to push past obstacles and access the resources you need to keep stepping forward. When you focus only on getting through, you miss the treasures that can be discovered along the way. If you continue to place more value on the end result than the growth process, the incredible riches of knowing God will always seem out of reach.

I have come to believe that the process is to be celebrated just as much as crossing the finish line. In fact, I believe that no matter what your calling is, what happens during the process is the preparation you need to fulfill it. You've probably experienced moments when a scripture you were reading became alive and took on a meaning that was relevant to a situation you were facing. It was as if the Spirit took a yellow highlighter and illuminated that passage to give you special understanding. This is called revelation or supernatural insight.

Here are two areas in which God wants to give you greater clarity as you embrace the process.

1. He will give you a clearer understanding of yourself. Through His process, and as your perception of yourself becomes clearer, your true beauty and worth will be revealed. Like the layers of an onion, God slowly peels back the barriers that have hindered you from seeing the real you, from embracing life more fully. Just as when we peel an onion and our tear ducts get activated, our emotions may get stirred, evoking deep feelings of sorrow and grief as we process all the pain that has been holding us back and keeping us stuck. At the same time, it will stir up tears of joy as we experience the freedom to let our true selves be known and expressed.

2. He will give you a clearer understanding of who He is. It is my experience that, with every opportunity you have to trust God, He reveals to you another aspect of His character so that you can know Him experientially and deepen the bonds of love and intimacy.

Throughout my life, I have had many opportunities to trust God to comfort me, but none like when I experienced the loss of my first husband. Before that, I had known that God was my comforter, but as I leaned into God to carry my pain and to comfort my aching heart, I came to know him as my Comforter. It's the difference between knowing in your head that God is your comforter and knowing in your heart that He is your Comforter.

When your knowledge is experienced at the heart level, no one can take that truth away from you. This is one of the greatest treasures you will take away from embracing the process: you will come to know God more intimately and become more deeply rooted in His love. With every opportunity to trust Him will come an increase in your ability to

> *understand, as all God's people should, how wide, how long, how high, and how deep his love is. May you experience the love of Christ, though it is too great to understand fully. Then you will be made complete with all the fullness of life and power that comes from God.*
>
> —Ephesians 3:18–19

As you draw near to God, gaining clarity about who He really is, you will experience a strengthening in the core of who you are. The foundation of your life will become stronger and keep you from crumbling when the storms of life hit. This foundation will empower you to stand firm when troubles come against you.

As mentioned before, the condition of your heart is more important to God than you living a perfect life outwardly. It's in your heart where He meets you and desires to connect intimately. With every invitation from Him to engage your heart is an opportunity to let Him expand your capacity to carry His presence in all His fullness.

In order to go to greater depths of intimacy with God and others, you need to be willing to trust that He is safe, good, and has your best interest in mind. Part of the Spirit's role is to lead you into truth and empower you to make the right choices so that you can be free to function as you were created to function. He may reveal distorted perceptions or unresolved issues in you, and invite you to receive the healing and deliverance necessary to become free. His goal is to transform you so that God's glory can shine through you, and you in turn can become an agent of transformation for others. Your role is to respond in humble obedience as the Spirit invites you to cooperate with Him in bringing about wholeness and freedom so the real you can step forward every day to walk in the fullness of your calling.

Your response will either entrap you or empower you.

This is the real power in embracing the process. You have a choice as to how your past will affect your present or your future. Your response will either entrap you or empower you. What you perceive to be true in the moment can be tainted by unresolved anger, bitterness, inner vows, and limiting beliefs.

One of the biggest obstacles that distorts people's perception is unforgiveness. The act of forgiving someone has profound implications that can move you from stuck to unstoppable, from bondage to freedom, and sometimes in a matter of minutes.

What keeps people from choosing to forgive is their lack of understanding about what forgiveness really is. Even though I briefly touched on forgiveness in a previous chapter, it's worth revisiting to deepen our understanding.

The Truth about Forgiveness

Many people find themselves stuck and unable to move forward because they aren't willing to forgive someone who has hurt them in the past. By holding on to unforgiveness, the soil of your heart becomes sterile and unable to produce good fruit in your life. Instead, it creates roots of bitter judgments, revenge, and clouded perceptions. Most people don't forgive easily primarily because they don't understand what true forgiveness really is. Forgiveness is an undeserved gift from God and an act of our will to extend that same gift to others.

When you choose to forgive someone, you're not saying that what they did was right or acceptable, nor are you excusing their behaviour. You are simply extending a gift that is undeserved, just like what Jesus extended to you. Forgiveness is more for your benefit than for the offender. By forgiving someone, you are taking away the control they have over you and releasing yourself to live free from its effects. You are simply handing them over to God to be their judge—because you are not their judge—and going on with life.

When you don't forgive someone, it creates an attachment, like an invisible rope, from your heart to their that restricts you from living your true self and fulfilling God's purpose for your life. Without realizing it, your decisions and movements become controlled by the other person's movements and choices.

For example, perhaps you really wanted to go to a particular restaurant, but you don't go because the person who hurt you goes there all the time and you're afraid that you may run into them. So you go somewhere else and allow that person to rob you of the enjoyment of eating there. Sadly, many people even give up their dream because of its negative association to someone they haven't forgiven.

Forgiving someone doesn't mean you need to trust them or be in relationship with them. Forgiveness is a gift whereas trust must be earned. You can't pay for a gift or earn one. Insisting that another person does something before you forgive them means that you're making them earn it, and that's an impossible task. If you're waiting for someone to apologize or acknowledge how they hurt you, or receive the punishment you think they deserve, then you're allowing them to control you by putting your life on hold. I like the way Ecclesiastes 11:4 puts it: *"Farmers who wait for perfect weather never plant. If they watch every cloud, they never harvest."*

Jesus illustrated the importance of not only saying the words but also forgiving from the heart (Matthew 18:35). Choosing to forgive someone is the first step, and as the forgiveness moves from mental assent to heartfelt compassion you can experience true freedom.

The Process of Forgiving

Heartfelt forgiveness is often a process in itself, and like any process you must choose to embrace it and allow God to take you through it to completion. At those times when I've found it difficult to forgive someone who hurt me deeply, I have imagined holding a box, a wrapped present in my hand that represents the gift of forgiveness God gave me for all the wrong things I've done in my life. As I make the choice to forgive and say, "I forgive (person's name) for how they hurt me," I extend my hand with the present in it and imagine giving it to the person I am forgiving. Then I ask God to enable my emotions to catch up to my choice, to actually *feel* forgiveness. Sometimes it takes months of praying this way until I feel forgiveness deep in my heart.

Perhaps this will help you if you struggle with forgiving someone, perhaps even with forgiving yourself. Forgiveness can be accomplished instantaneously, but the healing of the wound can be a longer process. The key is committing to the process for as long as it takes so that you can experience freedom and walk in wholeness.

You will know that you've truly forgiven from the heart when you:

- have feelings of compassion towards the offender.
- gain the ability to remember the incident without feeling the pain.
- desire to do good to the very people who hurt you.
- are no longer emotionally triggered by their words or actions.

Forgiveness is a powerful tool in your hands, both for your personal freedom and for cultivating deeper intimacy in your relationships. When I started to forgive my dad from my heart, it brought about changes in me, which in turn affected how he interacted with me. Within a short time after, he opened his heart to receive forgiveness and healing, and he experienced the power of Father God's love towards him as he chose to trust Jesus with his life.

In the latter part of my dad's life, we had a second chance to establish a father-daughter relationship based on love, safety, and truth. I now treasure those years of memories every time I think of my dad. Where once I felt hatred and bitterness, I now feel love and compassion. This is the power of forgiveness.

Stepping forward and experiencing the life Jesus came to bring will require us to believe that it's possible, and we will have to intentionally align our hearts to His so that we can walk in His ways. Having a clear vision for your life will lead to increased confidence, healthier relationships, and the courage to embrace the unlimited possibilities of kingdom living. This in turn allows you to accomplish more in less time as you learn to say no to things that don't line up with your true self or calling, and yes to those things that do.

You have an open invitation to partner with the Holy Spirit to create shifts in your thinking that transform how you see and do life, so that you can be free to live the real you and bring glory to God. Gaining clarity about who you are and your unique calling will empower you to not only step forward but also keep stepping forward in wholeness and freedom, and activating other people to do the same.

Stepping Forward

- Is there someone you still need to forgive from the heart?
- Take time to pray this prayer for each of the people who come to your mind: "I choose to forgive (person's name) for how you hurt

me. I extend this gift of forgiveness and say release you of all judgement I have made of you." Then make the motion of extending a gift to them (imagine you have one in your hand), as if they are right in front of you—and imagine giving it to the person you are forgiving. Then continue to pray this: "God, please enable my emotions to catch up to my choice, so that I can actually feel forgiveness towards (person's name)." Do this daily until it becomes a reality in your heart and you begin to see the person as God does and feel forgiveness in your heart for them.

• Journal your discoveries.

Endnotes

88   Burton, *Where Will You Go From Here?* 233–34.

Key #4

LIVE THE REAL YOU

———————————

People crave authenticity.[89]

—Eric Lokkesmoe and Jedd Medefind

chapter fifteen

The Courageous Heart

Those who have attained considerable spiritual stature are frequently noted for their "childlikeness." What this really means is that they do not use their face or body to hide their spiritual reality. In their body they are genuinely present to those around them.[90]

—Dallas Willard

In order to nurture connection in any relationship and be free to live the real you, it's essential that you believe that who you are is enough. As you show up ready to engage your heart, the fear of rejection, judgment, and feelings of shame will often surface to keep you from truly connecting with another. This is where you must remind yourself of this truth: you are enough. This is part of living in truth, living authentically.

According to *The Merriam-Webster Dictionary*, the word authentic is defined as "true to one's own personality, spirit, or character."[91]

Researcher and author Brené Brown conducted extensive studies on what characterizes authenticity and what gets in its way. She states that choosing authenticity includes "the daily practice of letting go of who you think you are supposed to be and embracing who you are."[92] From her research, she further concluded that living authentically demands wholehearted living and loving even when it's difficult. It requires a willingness to engage your heart no matter how painful the circumstance.

Whether you're dealing with shame, the fear of being rejected, or are bursting with joy and are afraid to fully express yourself, all are times to practice living the real you. When daily life is a struggle and the road ahead seems uncertain, that's the best time to practice being real. As you choose to be known and not cover up, you invite God's grace, joy, and love into your present situation.

Choosing authenticity isn't the easiest route, but it's the most rewarding. People closest to you may not like it when you choose to walk in truth, fearing how your changes will affect them. They may even try to make you feel guilty for being you. That's why it will take a courageous heart to live the real you. Living in truth involves embracing honesty, humility, and a willingness to let the real you be seen.

In her book *Rich Minds, Rich Rewards*, Valorie Burton says that once you set the intention to create a fulfilling life and begin to make the necessary changes, two things may happen.[93]

First of all, you may experience resistance from some of your family and friends who don't understand why you are living differently. Others will want you to stay as you are. They may not want you to move ahead because they fear being left behind and no longer included in your life.

The second thing that often happens is that you begin to attract people into your life with a similar mindset and values. As you take on a more positive attitude, you will attract positive people from whom you can learn and vice versa. Surrounding yourself with people who have a similar value system to yours will empower you to keep moving forward daily.

Authenticity is a powerful quality. It's very attractive, communicates strength and confidence, and can be very inspiring to others. It says, "This is who I am." It's about being honest about the struggles and trials you're facing but not getting stuck in that place. It requires you to courageously express who you really are even if others don't accept it or know how to be with you in that space. It doesn't mean making excuses for unhealthy ways of living; it does mean embracing who God created you to be. Living authentically is all about courageously living the real you.

The Merriam-Webster Dictionary defines courage as "mental or moral strength to venture, persevere, and withstand danger, fear, or difficulty."[94] When discussing the topic of courage, Brown adds that the root word *cour* comes from Latin, and it means "heart"; the original definition of courage meant "to tell the story of who you are with your whole heart."[95]

Throughout the Scriptures, God tells us to be strong and courageous and not to be afraid, knowing that God is with us. Courage is like a muscle that grows and expands with consistent use. The late Eleanor Roosevelt once said,

> You gain strength, courage, and confidence by every experience by which you really stop to look fear in the face. You are able to say to

yourself, "I lived through this horror. I can take the next thing that comes along."[96]

Living authentically will also involve taking risks. As you step forward, here are four types of risks you will need to consider taking:

- The risk of being rejected.
- The risk of being judged.
- The risk of being misunderstood.
- The risk of losing friends.

When I first became aware of how much God loved me, I decided to stop doing some activities I had previously done with friends. I realized that some of my actions were driven by my desire to fit in. As I began to live truer to who I really was at the core, some of my friends didn't understand and stopped calling me. Initially, it was tempting to go back to old habits, but the joy and peace I felt on the inside outweighed anything my old lifestyle could offer.

Your decision to live more authentically and intentionally will not go unnoticed. Your personal growth will evoke all kinds of responses around you. Some people will be excited for you while others will criticize and judge you. Still others will find it too uncomfortable and not stick around.

A fact worth remembering is that even private decisions can have an effect on other people, often for generations. That's why when you pray to change a response to a painful experience and extend forgiveness to someone, on a spiritual level the impact can be powerful. Those unseen choices will affect shifts in attitude and perspective and challenge others around you to make their own shifts.

A young girl named Catherine experienced this firsthand. She came to me for spiritual coaching and during our discussion discovered her need to break ties with a friend with whom she had made a blood covenant years earlier. As we talked, she realized that although it had seemed insignificant at the time, the commitment was controlling her life. That day, she chose to renounce the covenant and prayed to break the unhealthy attachments between them.

That very same evening, Catherine's friend phoned her from Asia and said, "What's going on with you? It feels like something has changed in our relationship." Indeed it had, and even though Catherine had said that prayer thousands of miles away in a private setting, her friend had felt the effect on the other side of the world. This interconnectedness is true in the spiritual realm as well as the emotional and physical realms. Your choices have power to affect significant change both in your own life and in the lives of others.

When I was grieving the loss of my first husband, confusion clouded my thoughts as I sought to process my pain as well as help my children process theirs. Every day was an attempt to establish a new normal for my family, to maintain stability and hope for our future. In the midst of my process, I sometimes felt misunderstood and judged. I was expending so much energy to care for the emotional and physical needs of my three children that sometimes I hardly had enough energy left to care for myself, let alone give to others.

Because I hadn't lost my confidence and was emotionally healthy (at least I thought I was), some people didn't understand why I wasn't available to engage in certain activities that I had been a part of before. That season led me to question whether life as it had been was supposed to continue. Some things had obviously and dramatically changed as I found myself widowed, a single parent with no family close by or stable income.

Immediately after the loss, the faith community generously supported us in whatever way they could, which was such a blessing for my family. But as life went on I needed to decide what the next chapter of our life would include. With our new normal not yet clearly defined in my heart and mind, the next season of our life was constantly in motion and filled with unknowns. In the midst of transition, it's common to experience confusion.

Letting Others Be in Process

Part of being authentic includes not only accepting without judgment the process of change in your own life but also in the lives of others. Supporting people in their process expresses honour, value, and love and says that you believe in them. Extending unconditional acceptance and loving accountability allows people the time they need to move through transition and live authentically. The danger is when we try to project onto others our idea of how the process should go, or how long it should take. Stepping forward as the real you doesn't mean that you always have your next steps clearly defined, but it does require that you continue to move forward in truth even when others misunderstand you.

Being spiritually strong and emotionally healthy doesn't mean you can quickly dismiss the painful emotions that accompany loss, betrayal, or other traumatic events. Nor do I believe you should. In my case, misunderstanding came when certain people viewed me as a strong person, which to them meant that I should get back to normal more quickly. The way they communicated with me during this period of change left me feeling like it wasn't okay for me to grieve or have difficult days; they thought I should just get back to doing what I had been doing before, especially in ways that benefited them.

As I turned to God for wisdom, I realized that the strength people saw in me was my spiritual condition. Over the years, God had established foundations of truth, trust, and peace in my life as I embraced transformation and learned how to be rooted and grounded in His love. So when I expressed vulnerability in a way that was unfamiliar to them, it put their perception of me into conflict and challenged their belief system. They couldn't reconcile how strength and vulnerability could coexist.

It is true that authenticity can sometimes be raw and others may not know how to respond to it. In her book *Daring Greatly,* Brené Brown describes the power of embracing our vulnerability and admitting our fears as a path that leads to being more courageous and connected to others. She suggests that this means letting go of the need for certainty and control. It means embracing the belief that we are enough and being willing to risk rejection and being misunderstood.[97]

Although I love the work of Brené Brown and agree with many of her perspectives, I don't agree that we are always enough. In and of ourselves, without the presence of God in our lives, we do not have what it takes to live the lives we are wired for. However, by His divine power, God has given us everything we need for living godly lives. We have received everything we need by coming to know Him and being in relationship with Him. So yes, as we live in Him, we are enough!

Embracing Imperfection

In admitting our imperfections, we open the door for God to be glorified. As we lean into Him to access everything we need, His strength empowers us to keep moving forward. Many people view vulnerability as a weakness, when in fact it's a posture of humility and honesty that carries with it the potential for great influence. Brown says, "Vulnerability sounds like truth and feels like courage. Truth and courage aren't always comfortable, but they're never weakness."[98]

As we saw previously in 2 Peter 1:3, when you get to know God His divine power flows through you, giving you everything you need to live who you were created to be. It's like having an all-season pass to God's heart and extravagant love. Everything you need can be accessed through relationship. So you are complete, lacking nothing, because of being spiritually connected to God. This doesn't guarantee that life will always be easy, but it does mean that you will never truly be alone nor helpless.

When faced with opposition, resist the urge to give up or hide. Instead, be strong and courageous, lean into God, and He will be with you every step of the way. Living authentically involves a risk: you have to make the choice every day to live the real you, no matter the situation. Living the real you is one of the best gifts you can give to those closest to you because it's rooted in truth and born out of the heart of God.

Authentic Prayers

Jesus lived authentically. One example of this was in the garden of Gethsemane, where Jesus let Himself be seen as vulnerable when He prayed to God the Father, pouring out His anxiety- and turmoil-filled soul. This is where living authentically must begin: in your relationship with God. He knows your heart anyway, so why not be honest with Him?

You also must risk being real in prayer in the presence of others, such as in a prayer group. This is about choosing to show up and be real, seeking to please God above anyone else. Experiencing

Choosing to open your heart and acknowledge your need for God is the first step to true freedom.

the freedom to be real in prayer will transfer into your everyday life relationships. Choosing to open your heart and acknowledge your need for God is the first step to true freedom. Surround yourself with people who are authentic and spiritually mature and who encourage you to not settle for less than all that God has for you.

Stepping Forward

- What scares you most about being authentic?
- What are you afraid will happen if you live authentically?
- How have you allowed fear to hold you back from being your true self?
- What one step of courage can you take today to start living the real you?
- Journal your discoveries.

Endnotes

89 Eric Lokkesmoe and Jedd Medefind, *The Revolutionary Communicator* (Lake Mary, FL: Relevant, 2004), 68.

90 Dallas Willard, *The Divine Conspiracy: Rediscovering Our Hidden Life in God* (San Francisco, CA: Harper & Row, 1998), 76.

91 "Authentic," *Merriam-Webster.* Date of access: June 26, 2018 (https://www.merriam-webster.com/dictionary/authentic).

92 Brené Brown, *The Gifts of Imperfection* (Center City, MN: Hazelden, 2010), 50.

93 Valorie Burton, *Rich Minds, Rich Rewards* (New York, NY: Villard Books, 2001), 80.

94 "Courage," *Merriam-Webster.* Date of access: June 26, 2018 (https://www.merriam-webster.com/dictionary/courage).

95 Brown, *The Gifts of Imperfection*, 12.

96 "14 Quotes on Courage to Help Conquer Your Fears," *Virtues for Life*. Date of access: June 26, 2018 (http://www.virtuesforlife.com/14-quotes-on-courage-to-help-conquer-your-fears/).

97 Brené Brown, *Daring Greatly* (New York, NY: Avery, 2012), 10.

98 Ibid., 37.

chapter sixteen

Common Blocks to Living the Real You

> If we can't stand up to the *never good enough* and *who do you think you are?* we can't move forward.[99]
>
> —Brené Brown

What's really holding you back from living true to who you have been created to be? Perhaps you're stuck because you don't know or even like yourself. Whenever I ask my clients to tell me who they are, they inevitably list off all the roles they play: "I'm a mother, a teacher, a wife, a businessperson…"

"No, *who* are you?" I ask again. "Those are the things you do, the roles you play. I want to know who you are at the core—the real you."

That's when most people become silent. Before you can live the real you, you need to know who the real you is! If you're like most people, past experiences have coloured your view of yourself. What you perceive to be true may actually be the wall you keep hitting as you attempt to move forward. Your perceptions form your belief system. The opportunities of life are viewed through your perceived truth, which include distortions, limiting beliefs, and lies. You may be surprised to hear that some of your perceptions may actually be deceptions.

The process I spoke about in the previous section is designed to help you see yourself from your Creator's eyes and to love your true self. This is the loving process God takes each of His children through as part of restoring us to a place of freedom, intimacy, and wholeness. Again, I want to remind you that you can't change what's happened to you, but you can change your response to what has happened.

One of the first requirements to embracing the process involves being willing to have your mindset challenged and perceptions shifted. This willingness creates openness in your heart to receive the truth and become aware of where your thinking may be based on distorted perceptions. This in turn makes room to understand the will of God for your life. You can pray as the psalmist prayed in Psalm 119:29: *"Keep me from lying to myself."*

Whenever you experience painful circumstances, your brain tries to figure out what it needs to do to maintain sanity and protect you. That's the primary function of the brain, to protect the body from harm. Our beliefs drive our decisions to act in certain ways. These ways of acting become habits and form our lifestyle. Living real includes becoming aware of how your current ways of thinking and acting may be holding you back from living in truth.

Over the years, I've discovered that there are at least four types of blocks that can prevent you from living the real you. There was a time in my life when all four of these blocks worked together to keep me from living true to myself. They are: fear, shame, comparison, and perfectionism.

Fear is something everyone can relate to, and shame is its close companion. Let's look at these together and learn how their influence can block you from living the real you.

Fear and Shame

When I first met Melanie, she seemed confident and outgoing. As I observed her in small group settings, I realized that she went to great lengths to avoid any kind of intimacy. Her friendships were superficial and based mostly on laughter and fun. In small group discussions, when others were sharing their hearts, she listened quietly and showed only controlled emotions. It took several years before she came to a point in her life where she wanted out. Hiding and maintaining control became too tiring and was taking a toll on her physically, as well as spiritually and emotionally.

When Melanie was younger, she had gotten involved in a relationship and ended up getting pregnant. Because she and her boyfriend were so young, her parents had insisted that she get an abortion, so she did. That abortion led to another, and yet another. Although it had been many years ago, the shame of what she'd done was still suffocating her. Even though she had continued to engage in premarital sex, she had vowed never to get too close to anyone, fearing they would only judge and reject her.

On some level, I could relate to Melanie. When I was a teenager, I had worked daily to hide my inner world, afraid to be seen, afraid to be known. From a young age, I had experienced events that led me to believe that I couldn't trust anyone, that it wasn't safe to allow anyone to get too close. I learned to protect myself by closing off my heart and walking around with masks covering my shame and hiding my pain and insecurity. The bitter judgments in my heart, the shame of family, and fear of the future prevented me from living true to who I really was.

As I sought to become someone else, I realized that I couldn't control the chaos around me, so I decided to take control of what I could: myself. I gradually developed disciplines to help me stay in control and searched for ways to numb my emotional pain. Instead of turning to alcohol and drugs, I found relief in what I now call a softer addiction: perfectionism, which was deeply rooted in the fear of being seen.

My teenage years were a difficult and tumultuous time for me, internally. However, it was also a pivotal season that changed the course of my life. While in the midst of my parents' divorce, I began to search for relief from the aching in my heart. My home environment had been filled with violence, rage, and abuse. Being religious, my family had taught me that following God was based on an external set of rules and doing enough good things to outweigh the bad. I discovered later that true Christianity is actually based on the internal condition of one's heart and having an intimate relationship with Jesus, who laid down His life so that I could be free to experience the fullness of God's love and life. It is this intimate, vibrant relationship that is meant to be the standard for all human relationships and the motivation for all we do.

Only when I took the risk of trusting God did my fears start to dissipate and my heart become free to live authentically. By engaging my heart, I learned a simple formula for breaking free of fear and shame. The book of 1 John 4:18 says that *"perfect love expels all fear"* and that there is no fear in true love. The more you live in love, the less you live in fear. As I chose to believe that God loved me unconditionally, and opened my heart to receive His love, fear's grip on my heart weakened.

You give power to that which you agree with.

Fear and shame make you try to cover up, hide your weaknesses, mask your pain, and harden your heart. They get in the way of giving and receiving love and prevent you from experiencing intimacy and meaningful connections. In her TED Talk, "The Power of Vulnerability," Brené Brown said that feelings of shame are actually rooted in a fear of disconnection and the belief that "if people see and know the real me, they won't consider me worthy of connection."[100] To give place to fear is to welcome its bondage and paralyzing effects.

Author Paula Rinehart affirms, "The movement of God in our lives is always to take us by the hand and walk us through the territory of our fear."[101] Why? Because as you courageously open your heart to let His love come in and trust in His hand to guide you, you will discover deeper levels of truth, intimacy, and freedom. These help form the basis for a richer, more fulfilling life.

Don't wait for the fear to disappear before stepping out. It's actually in the stepping out that fear is weakened. With every step comes a risk. It's who you put your faith in that's crucial. Are you placing your faith in what you can or can't do—or in who God is, and His promise to provide whatever you need in your moment of vulnerability? By courageously walking into fear and choosing to trust, I began to unleash the creativity and passion that lay dormant in my heart and experienced a new level of freedom.

In her book *Daring Greatly*, Brown warns, "To foreclose on our emotional life out of fear that the costs will be too high is to walk away from the very thing that gives purpose and meaning to living."[102] There's no way around it: you must walk through fear and leave it and shame in the dust as you step forward.

The Lure of Comparison

There was a time when I was complaining to God about why I had to endure certain things while other people seemed to have it much easier. I found myself comparing myself to others and their journeys. As I paused to listen for God's response, He directed me to read Psalm 73, in which King David vents his own complaints. As I read the passage, I realized that comparing myself to others had caused seeds of bitter resentment to take root in my heart. I had taken my eyes off what was important and been lured by the lie of comparison, which says that my life needs to be better than other people's lives. Perhaps this is what author Howard Hendricks meant when he said, "Comparison in the Christian life is a mark of carnality."[103]

As I continued dialoguing with God on this issue, I understood my situation from His perspective. I saw the bigger picture and understood why my life looked the way it did. He reminded me of when I had been in high school and part of the track team. He pointed out how my training regime had been different than my friend's because I was a long distance runner and she was a sprinter. Even though my friend and I were on the same team and had the same coach, our training had been designed to prepare us for our unique race and goals. I needed to train in such a way that developed endurance and strength to keep a consistent pace over ten kilometres, whereas she needed to develop her muscles to start her race quickly and maintain a fast speed for only a few hundred metres. If I had used her training regime to prepare for my races, I would never had lasted beyond the first two hundred metres, let alone finish. If I had done that, I might have come to believe that I wasn't a very good runner, and that belief might have prevented me from embracing my unique strengths and from successfully completing the race I was meant to run.

Unfortunately, this kind of comparison happens all too often, resulting in people getting stuck in their beliefs and eventually giving up on their dreams, and perhaps even life itself.

Your life's journey will look different than your friend's, because your mission and purpose is different. The track that lies ahead of you may require that you walk through certain experiences and develop different skills and disciplines in order to equip you to fulfill your unique purpose on the earth. The reality is that there will always be people who can do certain things better than you, and others who can't. You aren't meant to be like someone else; you are created to be you. A passage in Galatians wisely instructs you to compare yourself only to yourself and the progress you've made, because you are only responsible for your own behaviour:

Make a careful exploration of who you are and the work you have been given, and then sink yourself into that. Don't be impressed with yourself. Don't compare yourself with others. Each of you must take responsibility for doing the creative best you can with your own life.

—Galatians 5:4–5, MSG

In the adventure of life, you will not be judged according to how well you lived your life as compared to how someone else lived theirs. You will only be held accountable for whether you lived true to who you were designed to be, were faithful with what you were given, and whether you fulfilled your unique purpose. Compare yourself to yourself and how you have progressed and grown over the last year or month. Keep moving forward and living the real you.

The Trap of Perfectionism

Several years ago, I had the privilege of meeting Laurie Beth Jones, author, speaker, and life coach. Several of her books have had a profound influence on my life and helped instill courage in me to move out of my comfort zone and in a direction I sensed God leading me. In one of her books, *Jesus Entrepreneur*, Jones cited the Hebrew translation for the word "perfect," as found in Matthew 5:48: *"But you are to be perfect, even as your Father in heaven is perfect."* What she discovered is that the Hebrew translation for perfect is "compassionate."[104] Wow! I don't know about you, but when I read that it sure put a different spin on the meaning.

Jones believes that "the desire for perfectionism is a great excuse for staying stuck... Jesus was not a perfectionist. He knew that every picnic would have its flies and every person their flaws. He loved them anyway."[105] That's why the religious leaders got so mad at Him, because He didn't do everything perfectly according to the law or how they thought it should be done. The belief that you need to be perfect is one of the most dangerous lies to buy into and one of the biggest hindrances to living the real you. The perfectionist mindset is rooted in fear and driven by control. I know because I have experienced this trap firsthand.

Trying to be perfect also takes a lot of mental and emotional energy and leaves you feeling physically exhausted. When your goal is to be perfect, you aren't free to be the real you, because you're so focused on protecting your social image, hiding your secrets, or keeping your masks on. It's like trying to hold a balloon or beach ball underwater. No matter how hard you try, it just keeps popping up. My son, who was about six at the time, tried this in a swimming pool. As he tried to hold it underwater with his body, the ball kept throwing him off balance when it popped up. This is similar to what happens when you try to live a perfect life. Perfection is humanly impossible.

A perfectionist mindset says that if you don't do something perfectly, you won't be loved. It says that what Jesus did on the cross wasn't enough to make you acceptable and valuable. This mindset is rooted in fear and idolatry, exalting our own abilities above God.

Perfectionism prevents authentic and meaningful connections from occurring and limits your ability to walk in God's grace and righteousness. By striving to be perfect, you trust more in your own efforts instead of in the finished work of the cross. John speaks to this issue, saying, *"The Spirit alone gives eternal life. Human effort accomplishes nothing"* (John 6:63).

As a teenager, I became enslaved to addictive behaviours. I was ashamed to be associated with my family of origin and felt hurt by them. I was afraid of failing, being taken advantage of, and having my life turn out to be dysfunctional. So I decided that I was going to live differently and do things "the right way." This was the beginning of my quest for perfection. Eventually it led me to develop anorexia, an unhealthy independence, relational disconnection, and a hardened heart. Freedom came when I realized that nothing else could make me acceptable or worthy apart from the grace of God.

Many years ago, Linda Pender, a Christian counsellor, asked a question in one of her seminars: "What qualifies you for the blood of Jesus?" What she was really asking was this "How good do you have to be to be good enough for God to love and accept you?" Is it how well you perform, or how well dressed you are? Is it how many prayers you pray or good deeds you do? No, it's your *failures* that qualify you for the blood of Jesus. In other words, your imperfection qualifies you to receive the benefit of being in relationship with God.

The fact is that you and I are unable to get it right all the time. One of my favourite passages in the Bible is John 15, because it so beautifully depicts the reality that if you stay connected to God, your life will bear good fruit. However, if you depend solely on your own ability and strength, you will be frustrated, stuck, and unproductive.

In order to live the real you, you must believe that you're accepted just as you are and that you lack nothing because of your relationship with Jesus. People are attracted to strength, and when you try to be perfect people will be drawn to your false sense of strength, which only puts more pressure on you to keep up the façade and performance. When you accept your weaknesses and acknowledge that you can't do it by yourself, you make room for God to shine through your everyday life.

Choosing to live the real you means having the courage to let your imperfections be known. God is attracted to humility and vulnerability. Bringing strength to the weak is His specialty. He delights in empowering you, in making up for your inabilities by doing what you cannot so that you can move forward. The greatest secret of those who follow Christ is that His Spirit is alive within us and is ready to empower us at every turn, to help us live the lives we were created for. But first we have to let Him.

Breaking Free

Perfectionists try to have everything figured out before taking the next step. This often leads to mental paralysis and frustration. Walking in freedom means living a life of trust. Even though you may not have it all together or have all the answers, you choose to trust in God's ability to lead you. Only after you lay down your need to be perfect can you be truly perfected, or matured.

Instead of perfection, pursue connection. Lay down your need to be perfect and focus on living with a whole heart. Along the journey, value progress over perfection, and celebrate every new step you take as a victory towards wholeness and freedom.

As you yield your will and desire to God, He will teach you how to live in freedom and escape the trap of perfection. It starts with trusting that Jesus finished the work needed for you to be acceptable to God the Father, by His death and resurrection. There is nothing left to be added except acknowledging it and applying it to your life. Colossians 2:10 states that *"you also are complete through your union with Christ..."* The definition of the word "complete" includes "brought to its end, finished... wanting nothing necessary to completeness... perfect... that which is perfect... mature."[106] Therefore, when you are in Christ, you are already perfect, fully acceptable to God. As you connect your heart and spirit to God's, you will experience the strength and peace you long for, and it will flow without effort as you rest in Him as your basis of righteousness.

I don't want to convey the impression that living the real you is always easy. Engaging the heart and inviting others to look inside can be scary. However, I want to encourage you that as you push through the fear you will begin to experience peace, confidence, self-love, and the freedom to embrace the fullness of who you are designed to be. Cultivating a lifestyle of authenticity will involve courage, discernment, and deliberate choosing. Every day you will be faced with opportunities to live the real you over being someone else. The more you get to know Christ, the more you will discover the real you and be empowered to live in freedom.

Living the real you requires that you let go of perfectionism and pursue connection and fulness. Only then can you experience the rich, fulfilling life that's waiting for you.

Stepping Forward

- In what ways is your need to feel perfect keeping you stuck?
- What are you afraid will happen if you allow your imperfections to be seen?
- How is this hindering your spiritual growth?
- How is this hindering your relationship with others?
- What one way can you step forward today and trust God rather than your own efforts?

• Journal your discoveries.

Endnotes

99   Brown, *The Gifts of Imperfection*, 6.

100 Brené Brown, "The Power of Vulnerability," *TED*. June 2010 (https://www.ted.com/talks/brene_brown_on_vulnerability).

101 Rinehart, *Strong Women, Soft Hearts*, 167.

102 Brown, *Daring Greatly*, 33.

103 Hendricks, *Color Outside the Lines*, 73.

104 Laurie Beth Jones, *Jesus Entrepreneur* (New York, NY: Three Rivers Press, 2001), 220.

105 Ibid., 219.

106 "Teleios," *Bible Study Tools*. Date of access: June 26, 2018 (https://www.biblestudytools.com/lexicons/greek/nas/teleios.html).

chapter seventeen

Real Communication

Authentic communicators cut in the opposite direction. They strive to allow others to see and encounter things as they are.[107]

—Eric Lokkesmoe and Jedd Medefind

The increase in popularity of reality television suggests that our modern society is hungry for authentic, raw communication. People thirst for an encounter with the real. At a relationship level, your willingness to be real is essential to establishing trust and intimacy. If you find yourself consistently pushing back from vulnerability, your relationships will be shallow and unsatisfying. If you're in a leadership role, your influence and effectiveness will diminish if your communication lacks a certain degree of authenticity.

As a speaking coach, when a new client comes to me I take the time to get to know a bit about their personality first. In addition to coaching them on their message, I aim to also help them express their true self as they communicate. In the coaching process, they discover that merely sharing ideas and transferring knowledge isn't enough to influence an audience. Learning to speak with authenticity and passion is needed for a person to make a deeper connection and have a transformational impact on any audience.

Think about the speakers who have most impacted your life. What was it about them that touched your heart or ignited your spirit?

Jesus was explicitly authentic in how He communicated. He was real. He both delivered wise instructions and revealed a part of Himself in every interaction. Authors Eric Lokkesmoe and Jedd Medefind, in their book *The Revolution Communicator*, take an in-depth look at Jesus's communication style and suggest three qualities that made Jesus's communication particularly authentic. Let's look at each one separately.

1. He demonstrated vulnerability. Throughout the Scriptures, Jesus expressed a range of human emotions. When large numbers of His followers abandoned Him, He turned to His disciples and asked, "Will you leave me too?" (John 6:67) He wasn't embarrassed to reveal His heart to His friends, and at one time He begged them to stick close by. In the garden of Gethsemane, He expressed the anguish he felt within his heart. He said, *"My soul is crushed with grief to the point of death. Stay here and keep watch with me"* (Matthew 26:38).

Lokkesmoe and Medefind wrote,

> From first to last, Jesus allowed his true self to radiate through his communication—even those elements that might seem to diminish stature or nobility. This vulnerability did not dull his impact nor blunt his influence; it only made them brighter and sharper.[108]

2. He was direct and honest. Most artists depict Jesus as a meek and mild shepherd carrying a little lamb across His shoulders. Indeed, He is tender-hearted and gentle, but He is also strong-willed and fiercely focused. He had no difficulty confronting injustice and speaking his mind on matters he disagreed with. Medefind and Lokkesmoe point out that Jesus's harshest words seemed to be directed towards those who represented the opposite of authentic living. At times, His words were aimed to shatter the hardness of people's hearts, especially those belonging to the government and religious leaders. He invited people to follow Him, but He also explained to them what it would cost those who chose to take Him up on this offer. Other times His direct approach showed up in tender words soaked in unconditional love and grace. He was real and discerning as to how He needed to communicate in any given moment.

3. He was accessible. Many speakers today say what they need to say, greet a few selected listeners, and then get escorted out through a side door to avoid contact with their audiences. This is true of celebrities, politicians, and even some spiritual leaders. Jesus, however, modelled a more authentic approach; He walked, talked, and ate with the common people. There were times when He avoided the crowd, but not because He didn't want them to know Him.

He was especially accessible to His inner circle of disciples. Author Robert E. Coleman points out, "Amazing as it may seem, all Jesus did to teach these men his ways was to draw them close to himself. He was his own school and curriculum."[109] Jesus made Himself available to all people and even welcomed those who were considered social outcasts, rejected by most.

As you read the New Testament, you will see that this same style of authentic communication was duplicated in Jesus's disciples. You even see this woven throughout the Old Testament of Psalms and Prophets.

Contrary to what you may have believed, you are hardwired to live authentically and to express the real you in your everyday interactions with people. Authenticity is particularly powerful when it doesn't diminish the impact of what you want to communicate, but actually increases and enhances it.

When you open your life and invite others to see the real you, you help create a familiarity within you that promotes trust. When you choose authenticity over hiding behind masks, you open the door for love to flow through you, creating an atmosphere of safety and love, which leads to the possibility of transformational conversations. Dr. Joseph Umidi, author of *Real Talk*, believes that "the quality of your conversations is a barometer of the quality of your relationships."[110]

By engaging in authentic communication and transformational conversations, you strengthen and expand your chances to impact others, activate life-changing breakthroughs, and help others through mentoring and loving support. By engaging in authentic conversations, you create a pathway to deeper intimacy and promote transformation in the following four ways.

1. Healing and reconciliation. As you choose to face your vulnerability and acknowledge what you're really feeling, you create space for healing to occur. Medefind and Lokkesmoe believe that "authenticity is the first step in healing."[111] The gospel is all about reconnecting people's hearts to God and to each other. This is what 2 Corinthians 5:18 refers to when it says that we have all been given the ministry of reconciliation. These authors also believe,

> Those who are committed to authentic communication consistently give names to the feelings, sensations, and experiences others have known but have never uttered. Inevitably, such communication touches both hearts and minds, knitting us to others with an intimacy we have never before experienced.[112]

As you learn to live the real you, the way you communicate will changes and you conversations will become more transformational.

2. Trust. As you engage your heart when interacting with others, you invite them to look closer at who you really are. This creates safety and helps build trust. As people see that your authenticity isn't just in words but also in your actions, it promotes an atmosphere of trust. Living authentically involves having conversations that go beyond simple communication to meaningful connections. Medefind and Lokkesmoe add that this also involves going beyond trying to avoid lies to intentionally expressing the whole truth, no matter how uncomfortable, vulnerable, or inconvenient it may be.[113] When you allow yourself to be seen in this way, it helps create integrity and paves the way for deeper intimacy.

3. Growth and transformation. Having authentic conversations isn't just about what you say. It's also about how you make the other person feel. Our normal conversations are usually transactional, focused more on getting information from each other or trying to make something happen. Dr. Umidi says that the purpose of transformational conversations "is to empower others to reach their fullest potential, improve their quality of life and achieve their dreams."[114] The power of authentic communication is that it makes room for growth and mindset shifts to occur in a single conversation. Dr. Umidi said that

> the power of such transformation goes beyond the immediate changes it creates. By fostering transformation in others, you are helping them create an entirely new way of being, as well as allowing them to see for themselves the power of developing rich connections with others.[115]

I have experienced some amazing benefits over the years of encouraging transformation in others. Sometimes it even causes more transformation to occur in my own life. As you choose to live the real you, you will develop stronger relationships and learn to care about and believe in those around you more deeply.

4. Transformational conversations. The word "conversation" comes from a Latin word which means "changing together."[116] I believe it is possible for every conversation to be life-imparting, life-impacting, or life-igniting. Dr. Umidi captures the original Latin meaning by referring to these types of conversations as transformational conversations. He describes them as ones that "create a real and powerful connection with others on a level that generates breakthroughs, inspires change, and enriches your relationships."[117] How would your relationships be different if you dared to cultivate such types of conversations on a daily basis? The focus of transformational conversations is to celebrate each other rather than simply interact with each other. When you engage at this level, you become

> I believe it is possible for every conversation to be life-imparting, life-impacting, or life-igniting.

a catalyst for change and empower people to realize what Umidi describes as their "fullest capacity for joy and personal growth."[118]

In an earlier chapter, I mentioned my friend Keiko and the impact she had on my life simply through the way she interacted with me. Throughout our friendship, I learned how to lay down my agenda in conversations with others and seek to listen more attentively with my heart. Through Keiko's life, I discovered how even the briefest interaction can have deep, lasting impact. And that breakthrough may only be one conversation away.

Blocks to Real Conversations

Living authentically requires courage and a commitment to living true to the real you. It also requires a commitment to create non-judgmental spaces in conversations where others can feel safe and accepted to be real as well. It has been said that the quality of your conversations will determine the quality of your relationships. Therefore, as you take steps to improve the quality of your conversations, you strengthen your relationships. Becoming aware of what inhibits authenticity is the first step in creating change in how you communicate.

Dr. Umidi warns that there are actions and situations that "shut people down, shut them out or just plain shut them up."[119] If you engage in these actions, you will derail meaningful connections and settle for conversations that leave you feeling drained, depressed, or defeated. These actions, which the author refers to as conversation killers, can end up costing you opportunities for significant growth, intimate connections, and profound transformation. During an online program hosted by Compass Life Designs, Dr. Umidi outlined a number of these conversation killers. Here are a few items from his list.

Unsolicited advice. When you impose your needs and advice, it steers the conversation away from what the other person really wants and needs. This conversation killer is all about you, what you want to give, or what you think the other person needs. Behaving this way in conversations is often reflective of your own discomfort with the person's distress and your need to try to fix the problem. Lasting transformation happens when a person is part of the process of uncovering the solution to their own problems, through revelation or meaningful connection. Thus transformational conversations are more about empowering the other person to find a path to his or her own solution. When you give unsolicited advice, you're offering your own solutions; in transformational conversations, you're empowering others to take responsibility for accessing their own solutions.

This is a skill you can learn. A well-trained coach can help in this area by asking you the right questions.

Agendas. Dr. Umidi defines this conversation killer as the "personas, purposes and intentions that you bring to the conversation that prevents you from seeing what's really there."[120] While he admits that it isn't possible to become completely agenda-free, the key "is to become aware of what your agendas are in any conversation so you can keep them from blocking your opportunity to make a difference."[121] There is a time and place for agenda-based conversations; however, if that's all you have, you'll miss out on the experience of intimately connecting with someone's heart and spirit. It is in these types of connections where the true power and strength of relationships are found. How you interact with others says a lot about you. The quality of your relationships will provide insight into the condition of your heart and the degree of freedom and wholeness you walk in.

Unconscious judgments. The third type of conversation killer is what Dr. Umidi refers to as unexamined judgments. These are unconscious beliefs you hold about someone that block you from seeing who they really are. You relate to them based on the labels you hold in your mind, which may or may not be accurate. These can be formed because of previous experiences with them, or possibly experiences you've had with someone they resemble who left messages written on your heart and unresolved issues, which can lead to forming distorted perceptions.

Sometimes you may have an issue that has nothing to do with the person you're conversing with. Instead you're projecting your judgment onto them because they remind you of someone from your past. Recognizing that it's virtually impossible to be totally judgment-free, make it your goal to at least become aware of these judgments and compare them against what's really true. Often this will require you to put aside your preconceived perceptions long enough to get to know the real person and learn the truth. As you approach the relationship with an open heart, you may be surprised to find that they have more endearing qualities than you expected.

Verbal villains. These conversation killers are personalities that shut down discussion. For example, a verbal villain may be someone who changes the subject when you get too close or touch on heart issues, or maybe they redirect the topic to focus on their own achievements. They may deliberately distract you from a topic to avoid intimacy. Excessive humour is a common detour tactic. Sometimes a person jumps from one random topic to the next in an attempt to stay in control of the conversation and avoid being seen for who they really are.

As you learn to engage your heart, embrace the process of transformation, and expand your capacity to give more love, authenticity will show up in how you communicate with others.

There are qualities that need to be at the forefront of all your interactions with others. As you have compassion in walking through the process, you will naturally extend compassion to others and cultivate a heart that's characterized by these three things.

1. Unconditional love. This isn't an easy approach, especially when you encounter people you don't know or like. As you engage in conversations, it's important to keep in mind what Umidi said: "maintaining a posture of unconditional love is all about who you are and not who they are."[122] That means that you put no conditions put on the other person whatsoever. You are simply "holding that space within yourself for whoever shows up."[123]

What comes to mind when you imagine yourself doing that? I think it's important to note here that unconditional love doesn't give others license to treat you however they want without expecting a consequence, nor does it mean that you won't need to protect yourself in hurtful situations. Trust and love are two separate postures. You can love someone unconditionally without trusting his or her actions. Trust must be earned.

By the same token, without self-love you will find yourself in relationships with people who are needy and overly dependent. Author Valorie Burton believes that "once you discover your own true self-love, you are then able to give love unconditionally to the significant people in your life."[124]

2. Respect. To live the real you and allow others to do the same, you need to make room for mutual respect to develop and be reflected in your conversations. This is linked to the ability to love yourself and others unconditionally. This means being mindful of not only what you say but also how you make others feel as a result of them interacting with you.

3. Honour. To promote authentic living, you need to cultivate a habit of honouring yourself and others. Dr. Umidi says that honouring someone means to "recognize who they truly are and nurture that truth."[125] I see it as celebrating their unique personhood. The first person you need to honour is God. As you give God first place, honouring Him above all else, your ability to honour yourself and others will become easier, as a by-product of your intimacy with God.

Stepping Forward

- How can you change the level of conversation in your daily life from focusing on information to transformation?
- How are you allowing your agenda, habits, or judgments to prevent you from engaging in authentic communication?
- What step can you take today to show honour towards the people you converse with?
- Journal your discoveries.

Endnotes

107 Lokkesmoe and Medefind, *The Revolutionary Communicator*, 71.

108 Ibid., 75.

109 Robert E. Coleman, *The Master Plan of Evangelism* (Grand Rapids, MI: Revell, 1993), 41.

110 Dr. Joseph Umidi, "The Power of Transformational Conversations," *Compass MAP™ Coachcast*. December 6, 2009. From a *Real Talk* training podcast called "Discover the Power of Transformational Conservations, My Life Compass: Compass MAPS,™" December 6, 2010.

111 Lokkesmoe and Medefind, *The Revolutionary Communicator*, 79.

112 Ibid., 82.

113 Ibid., 80.

114 Dr. Joseph Umidi, "The Power of Transformational Conversations," *Compass MAP™ Coachcast*. December 6, 2009.

115 Ibid.

116 Ibid.

117 Ibid.

118 Ibid.

119 Ibid.

120 Ibid.

121 Ibid.

122 Ibid.

123 Ibid.

124 Burton, *Rich Minds, Rich Rewards*, 158.

125 Dr. Joseph Umidi, "The Power of Transformational Conversations," *Compass MAP*™ *Coachcast*. December 6, 2009.

Key #5

EXPRESS YOUR UNIQUENESS

———————————

The measure of a life, after all, is not its duration but its donation.[126]

—Corrie ten Boom

chapter eighteen

Discovering Your Uniqueness

You don't have to fight your way into the presence of good partners and successful people. All you have to do is identify and build up your gifts. Your gifts will make room for you and bring you into the presence of great people.[127]

—T.D. Jakes

"That is breathtaking," my friend Dani said as she looked at the brightly lit display of colour dancing in wavy motions in the northern Alberta night sky. I had only read about the aurora borealis phenomenon, and now I was witnessing its sparkling beauty for myself.

"Let's pull over and get out! I want to see more," said our friend Kirk from the backseat.

"Great idea," I said as Dani pulled off the road.

All three of us quickly got out of the car and stood in wonder, looking up at the majesty and mystery of God's creativity in motion.

That's just like you! You are a product of God's love, created by Him with a combination of talents, strengths, and passions that are unique to you. As you learn to dance through life more freely from a place of uniqueness, you will display the brilliance of God's glory and others will want what you have. Your purpose will become clearer as you lean into your strengths and live more honestly from your heart.

A mosaic of divine creativity can be seen throughout nature. For example, each snowflake is uniquely designed, no two being alike. The same is true with your fingerprints. Even the iris of your eye is said to reveal something distinct about you. There is also some research to suggest that your voice has a specific "print" that distinguishes it from everyone else's.

When you were formed in your mother's womb, you were fashioned for a purpose and endowed with a mixture of gifts and strengths that are unique to you. Many people spend their whole lives trying to figure out what they are to do as a career or calling. I believe that if you focus on knowing God and embrace who you are, you will start to understand how you are wired. As you begin to function in your areas of greatest strength and offer your uniqueness to serve others, you will find yourself doing what you were designed to do without realizing it. Unless you learn to live authentically, you will lack deep fulfillment and never experience what author Kim George calls your "greatness capacity."[128]

You have the ability to make a significant impact in the world. If you have the Spirit of God living in you, you have an extraordinary capacity. Many scientists claim that you and I use only a small percentage of our brain's capacity. I believe this is also true of our heart's capacity.

The Apostle Paul said it well: *"Christ lives in you. This gives you assurance of sharing his glory"* (Colossians 1:27), *"It is no longer I who live, but Christ lives in me"* (Galatians 2:20), and *"But with God everything is possible"* (Matthew 19:26). If God is your ultimate source, you have unlimited abilities available to you (Ephesians 3:16–17). What you have to offer is not only valuable but also essential to pass on.

Authors Jedd Medefind and Eric Lokkemode invite us to ponder this question: "After all, what else besides our own realness do we have to offer that is truly unique- distinct, matchless, and thoroughly authentic?"[129]

As you embrace the process of transformation, you may need to rediscover who you really are, or your perception of yourself. If you've experienced loss, disappointment, or setbacks, you may also need to redesign your life or create a new normal, as I did. Transformation involves change and change requires shifts in how you think and act.

To successfully step forward and live true to your unique self, you will need to be willing to shift in the following ways.

Shift from confusion to clarity. As you step forward to engage your heart, embrace change, and express your unique self, you will gain new clarity about your true identity. This will lead you to an awareness of what resonates as truth inside you and what influences come from your external world. The outside influences usually stem from one of three main categories: roles, relationships, and rewards.

In the past, you may have defined yourself according to the roles you played, such as a parent, wife, husband, leader, or teacher. When you experience the loss of a job or any other role change, you may find yourself in a state of confusion.

I want to encourage you to see it for what it is: something you do. It's not the essence of who you are.

Similarly, you may have defined yourself by the relationships you had or the people you were surrounded by. When those people move away or the nature of a relationship shifts, it can be jarring to your identity.

Lastly, some people have built their self-worth and identity on what they have accomplished or earned, or on the praise of others. The rewards of life are never meant to define who you are. You are far more than the sum of these things. Understanding where you find your value and worth is essential in promoting clarity when it comes to your identity and the unique offering you bring to the world.

As you come to understand more about who you are at the core, you will experience some discomfort—and perhaps confusion. This is normal and no reason to stop moving forward. Take the time to identify any aspects of your uniqueness that you decided to bury after being misunderstood by significant people in your life. Invite God to bring healing and breathe life back into those areas so that you can fully embrace those unique qualities as part of the real you. Seek to embrace your true identity which is found in relationship with Christ.

> Your circumstances may have changed, but who you are is still intact.

Shift from uncertainty to confidence. Processing grief led me to process other losses surrounding my spouse's death. In addition to the loss of my role as a wife and ministry partner, I also experienced the loss of many relationships. Many people whom I considered friends either vanished or distanced themselves. I hadn't expected such dramatic changes, so in addition to being confused this affected my trust and confidence in those relationships.

As I conversed with God about these painful shifts, He comforted me with these words: "Your circumstances may have changed, but who you are is still intact. Your future will look differently than you imagined, but your gifts and your calling have not changed. Keep doing what I called you to do." Remembering this truth me focused on moving forward.

In her book *Where Will You Go from Here?* Valorie Burton echoed this when she said, "*What* you are may have changed but *who* you are remains constant."[130]

When you experience shifts in your thinking, or shifts in what was once normal, you need to have faith that you can make the transition. Keep in mind that it's not about what you lack but rather about knowing who loves you; that's what will make the difference in your life. The key is in what you do today, not what you know about tomorrow.

Burton described what I walked through in terms of evaluating the relationships in my life:

> Though the loss of any relationship is unfortunate, their decision frees you to enjoy truly authentic relationships with those who love you for who you are at your core, not what you do or what you do for them.[131]

Your confidence will grow as you shift your focus away from what you no longer have to what you never lost. Focus on what remains: your true self, your faith in God, your closest relationships, and the completeness that comes from being spiritually connected to God.

Shift from fear to courage. This type of shift will involve your willingness to embrace new possibilities. You will experience the tension between fearing the unknown and the desire to experience more. First of all, it's important not to force the shift prematurely, but to embrace the process as it unfolds. Moving forward and offering your uniqueness to others will require you to evaluate what is, what was, and what is to be. You may be challenged every step of the way in what you believe to be true about God, yourself, your future, and about what you need to engage life wholeheartedly.

Resist the tendency to go back to life as it was. As you learn to express the real you more consistently, carefully consider each commitment and relationship you add to your life. In order to offer the world the best of you, your actions will need to be aligned with Him. When fear tries to paralyze you, remind yourself of these truths: God is on your side, you have access to everything you need to step forward, and who you are in Christ is enough for you to succeed. As I've often heard Kim George say, "It's not what you can't do, but doing what you *can* do."

Courage is not the absence of fear but the ability to act through fear. It takes courage to live the real you, and courage is a thing of the heart. I love how the Oxford Dictionary describes courage: "strength in the face of pain or grief."[132] In other words, courage is about having the strength to live from the heart when fear tries to hold you back.

Where do you get that strength? The J.B. Phillips translation of Colossians 1:11–12 suggests that strength comes from being spiritually connected to God:

As you live this new life, we pray that you will be strengthened from God's bound-less resources, so that you will find yourselves able to pass through any experience and endure it with courage. You will even be able to thank God in the midst of pain and distress because you are privileged to share the lot of those who are living in the light. (Phillips)

Who Are You Really?

Stepping into the real you will require that you become aware of what's true for you and your unique calling. Apart from knowing your identity as a child of God, discovering your uniqueness involves identifying your values, passions, strengths, and personality. You also need to examine your life to see if the way you live aligns with and reflects your truth in these areas.

Let's take a look at each area separately.

Values. In addition to one's moral values, people usually operate out of a second set of values unique to them. These are their non-negotiables and are often undergirded by spiritual values. For example, if you value weekly family time, then choosing to take a job that will keep you away from your family a lot doesn't support that value. To take that job would move your actions out of alignment with your core values.

As a young believer, I learned that an essential aspect of loving someone is allowing him or her the freedom to choose. I believe that one of the gifts God gave us is the power to exercise free will. 1 Corinthians 13:5 says that love *"does not demand its own way."*

When I was in my early twenties, I dated a man named Bruce. Around this same time, I was growing a lot spiritually and my beliefs about love and relation-ships were being challenged. Bruce said that he was a believer, except he didn't really practice what he said he believed.

At different points in the relationship, I felt little twinges inside. I kept thinking, *Something isn't right.* Because I mostly felt happy when I was with Bruce, though, I ignored those twinges—that is, until one day when I felt a prodding in my heart that almost ripped my insides out.

I had been working as an assistant for one of my university professors and had just spent a few hours going over some projects with him. Afterward, Bruce and I went for lunch and I mentioned that I really liked working with this profes-sor and thought he was a nice man.

Almost instantly, Bruce looked up from his coffee and stared straight into my eyes from across the table. "I don't want you to spend any more time with him," he said, firmly.

"Why?" I asked after a moment of shock and silence. "He's my boss."

"I don't like him. I don't think it's safe for you to spend time with him."

I left that conversation feeling stunned, and realizing that Bruce was jealous for no good reason. He was very possessive of me. I had seen glimpses of this before, but nothing this blatant. I was familiar with this kind of behaviour, because my dad had been like that with my mom in the early stages of their marriage.

Shortly after that, I broke up with Bruce. Even if he was only a tiny bit controlling and possessive of me, that was a tiny bit too much and I thought that it would eventually become an all-consuming problem. I would not be free to be me.

I'm so glad that I didn't ignore the warning signals my heart was sending me that day. I had been learning to pay attention to my heart, and that day I made a choice based on two of my core values: freedom and trust. Even though Bruce was nice in other ways, staying in that relationship would have eventually choked the life out of me and violated my core values.

You can find many tools on the internet to help you to more thoroughly explore your core values. Here's a simple exercise to get you started in your discovery. Of the list of words below, choose the top ten that resonate with you, the ones that represent your non-negotiable values. Then refine it even further by choosing your three strongest values out of those ten.[133]

Truth	Compassion	Authenticity
Trust	Fairness	Simplicity
Integrity	Optimism	Clarity
Freedom	Fun	Order

Generosity	Love	Excellence
Service	Security	Harmony
Loyalty	Relationships	Productivity

Passions. The words passion and desire are profound expressions of the heart. Unfortunately, they are often seen as having a negative, unholy connotation. As a result, many Christians try to downplay their passions and desires out of the fear that they might be judged as carnal and compromising.

I believe that Christians should be the most passionate people on the earth because we are made in the image of God, who is extremely passionate about life and love. When you align your heart and mind to God's, your desires will begin to reflect His. As you seek to know and experience Him, your heart will become awakened and alive with passion and the desire to live more fully.

To clarify, there is a distinction between temporary urges for pleasure and godly desires, and you need to be able to discern the difference. Aligning your actions to your passion requires an awareness of those activities or aspirations that evoke life and joy in the deep places of your heart and mind. To be passionate about something means caring deeply about it, putting your whole heart into it, and deriving great joy and fulfillment from it.

Here are a few questions to ask yourself to help identify what you are passionate about:

- If you could do anything in the world, what would you do?
- What activities do you engage in that leave you feeling energized both during and after they're over?
- What topics or ideas make you "light up" when you talk about them with others?

As you embrace the real you and pursue fullness of life, it will be wise to monitor how the pursuit affects you each step of the way. Does it bring you temporary happiness and satisfaction, or does it feed a deep, abiding joy and sense of fulfillment? Does it leave you feeling energized and inspired? Or does it leave you feeling drained and depleted?

I found a plaque several years ago that had this anonymous quote on it which I think captures what passion is all about: "There are many things in life that will catch your eye, but only a few that will catch your heart… pursue those!"

The other two aspects of your unique offering to the world—your strengths and your personality—will be discussed in the next chapter.

Stepping Forward

- Take the time to discover your unique set of values. List your top three.
- What things do you do now that ignite your spirit and leave you feeling strengthened after engaging in them?
- What things do you keep thinking about and wish you could be involved in more?
- List the ways in which your life currently reflects your values and passions. If it doesn't reflect them, why not?
- What one action step can you take to start aligning your life according to your values and passions?
- Journal your discoveries.

Endnotes

126 Criswell Freeman, *Purpose for Everyday Living: Finding God in Your Everyday Life* (Nashville, TN: Thomas Nelson, 2004), 147.

127 T.D. Jakes, "T.D. Jakes Ministries," *Facebook*. July 19, 2014 (https://www.facebook.com/bishopjakes/posts/10152740941903322).

128 Kim George, *Coaching into Greatness: 4 Steps to Succeed in Business and Life* (Hoboken, NJ: Wiley, 2006), 63.

129 Lokkemode and Medefind, *The Revolutionary Communicator*, 90.

130 Burton, *Where Will You Go From Here?* 143.

131 Ibid., 150.

132 "Courage," *Oxford Living Dictionaries: English*. Date of access: June 26, 2018 (https://en.oxforddictionaries.com/definition/courage).

133 For a more extensive list of values and a worksheet to help you align your life around your values, go to www.lisavanderkwaak.com/realyou.

chapter nineteen

Embracing Your Uniqueness

Yet God is calling each of us to find, and live, his or her authentic voice.[134]

—Laurie Beth Jones

Have you ever taken a personality test? There are many personality assessments available, and I've done quite a few over the years. The one I love the most is called the Path Elements Profile™ (PEP™ for short),[135] which was developed by Laurie Beth Jones. It's a fantastic tool for identifying individual strengths and training teams and leaders in more effective communication and dynamic performance. The PEP™ is used widely and is an excellent tool for large and small organizations. It's simple to complete and easy to remember. At a training conference in 2009, I heard Jones say that the PEP™ is highly intuitive and a powerful tool that is "simple, sound, sticky and spreadable." She also claims that "it helps to clarify your motivations, values, likes/dislikes and a list of tendencies for how you work, play, lead, negotiate, take action, solve conflict, handle relationships, complete tasks, socialize and several more."

What makes the profile so "sticky," or easy to remember, is that personality types are described according to four elements found in nature: earth, wind, water, and fire. The uniqueness of your personality is defined by your strongest element and a complementary element as well as a score based on a scale revealing your element intensity.

For example, my PEP™ report says that I am a Wind-Fire personality. What that means is that my score in the Wind and Fire areas are within the same range, indicating that I function equally strong in both.

Thinking of the characteristics of the wind, what comes to mind? In nature, wind is an instrument of change. It doesn't move in a straight line and it provides energy, force, and life. Also, its presence is known by its impact on its surroundings. For example, you can only see wind when it blows on objects in its path, such as a tree. Wind can be fast or slow, gentle or powerful, and it helps move things from one place to another. It can even change directions without effort, and it's a necessary part of growth and development in nature.

Now, how does that relate to me? I'm passionate about helping others embrace change and get from one place to another. One of my friends has described me as an "iron fist in a velvet glove," meaning that when I speak or coach, I help people shift their mindsets and life in a strong but gracious manner. The strength of the fist (fire) is seen only when it makes contact with someone or something. The wind aspect of my personality helps soften the impact; it's like a velvet glove. This is how God wired me. I'm honoured and humbled to have influenced others in that way.

All the four elements are powerful in their own way and need to be tempered so as to bring life and not destruction. Staying close to God's heart is essential to tempering your strengths so that when you operate in them, you experience the positive impact instead of the potentially negative one. This same tension is found in each of the personality types.[136]

Unique Design

You were divinely fashioned in your mother's womb, no matter the circumstances surrounding your conception. You were wired with a specific purpose in mind. Gaining an appreciation and understanding for your unique personality and learning to walk more consistently in your strengths is key to letting the real you step forward to fulfill your purpose.

Many people focus on fixing their weakness, believing that somehow that's an important part of improving themselves. However, I want to encourage you not to do that. Focusing on your strengths will grow you more, moving you closer to a life characterized by fulfillment and joy. The opposite is also true. If you focus on overcoming weaknesses, your weaknesses will grow and expand, leading to frustration. Instead, lay your weaknesses and imperfections before God and ask Him to empower you to live from the place of your true identity.

I once heard Lance Wallnau ask, "Do you understand that your gifts, your talents, your abilities, your acquired skills, under the anointing are designed to meet a need no one else can meet like you?… Your excellence is in the things you do that no one else can compete with."

Author Marcus Buckingham interviewed one hundred of the most success-ful and happiest women in a certain group to find out what they did differently than other women. He outlined his findings in his book, *Find Your Strongest Life: What the Happiest and Most Successful Women Do Differently.* His research revealed that the most successful women don't live balanced lives but rather strive for im-balance. The secret to their success and fulfillment lay in their ability to do lean into their "strength-zone."[137] What this means is that they deliberately focused on things in life that allowed them to function in the areas of their greatest strengths.

Buckingham went on to define a strength as "an activity that makes you feel strong" during and after engaging in it.[138] You usually look forward to doing it, and afterward you feel more authentic, connected to your core, and functioning at higher levels of awareness. You feel like you're in your zone, in the sweet spot.

One day, my husband, David, observed that I looked refreshed after spend-ing the day teaching and leading a coaching group.

"You must really enjoy teaching others," he said. What he was observing was that empowering and coaching others left me feeling energized and vibrant. It may leave someone else feeling drained and weakened. A weakness, then, is defined simply as an activity that depletes your energy, motivation, and drive.

It is important here to distinguish between performance and fulfillment. You may have performed a task well, but if it drained your energy or made you lose your concentration, then according to Buckingham it's a weakness. Can you think of a few activities in your life right now that fit this description?

Several years ago, I was teaching a church course on a topic I'm passionate about: transformation. After a session, one of the participants came up to me and said, "Wow, I'm enjoying seeing you functioning in your element." I knew what she meant. Previous to taking this course, she had only observed me leading in an-other ministry department; I performed well there, but it wasn't in my strength-zone. It didn't give me life like this area did. What she was now observing was the difference between simply working in a job and walking in my joy!

Even though others may tell you what they observe you to be good at, ul-timately *you* are the best judge of your strengths. Only you know what effect certain activities have on you and what breathes life and vitality into your be-ing. Friends who are intuitive will pick up on times when you seem more alive than others, but they may not know why. This "aliveness" is often a clue to your strengths and passions.

Even though we need people to affirm what we do best, you are the best judge of what brings you life in the deepest part of your core. Proverbs 14:10

speaks to this truth when it says, *"Each heart knows its own bitterness, and no one else can fully share its joy."*

To help you gain greater clarity and confidence and grow in courage about living the real you, here is a four step process that I developed called the Four A's of Embracing Your Uniqueness.

1. Awareness. The first step towards any change is awareness. To embrace your uniqueness, you must first become aware of what it is you are embracing. Your uniqueness consists of a combination of your values, passions, strengths, and experiences. You can ask yourself some questions in order to become more aware of the unique mix you bring to the world.

As for values, what things are non-negotiable in your life? As to passions, what are some areas of life that awaken your soul, cause a fire to stir in you, and motivate you to take action? In terms of identifying your strengths, what seems to come naturally to you and leaves you feeling invigorated? What is confirmed through personality assessments or friends who point out what you're good at? How have your experiences shaped you and prepared you for certain opportunities you face today? How can you add value to someone else's life because of the authority you carry in areas in which you have overcome in life?

2. Acceptance. Once you become aware of these aspects that make you unique, it's important that you own them. Accept your uniqueness as part of how you are designed to function and treat them as part of your greatest asset. This involves embracing who you are and believing that you have been created this way for an important reason. You will also need to accept that some kind of change will be necessary if you are to keep moving forward. Whether it involves changing your habits, your current social network, or how you talk to yourself, you need to be willing to accept change as part of the process of transformation and becoming free to live the real you.

3. Aligning your focus. This will require making some bold decisions to restructure where you focus your time, energy, and money so that you're consistently leaning into your areas of greatest strength and expanding your capacity. You will need to let go of the things that don't line up with what's true for you and deliberately say no to certain things to make room for things that are in alignment with your strengths, values, passions, and unique calling.

4. Action. Buckingham's research revealed that the women he interviewed became the happiest and most successful when they started living *imbalanced* lives. This is what it will take to embrace your uniqueness and to step forward into the real you.

Many years ago, I realized that trying to live a balanced life was impossible. Think of an old-fashioned balancing scale. When items of equal weight are placed on both sides, the scale is perfectly balanced. When this happens, note that scale doesn't move. So, to live a truly balanced life, you need to ensure that nothing in your live moves or changes.

But real life isn't like that; it's dynamic, always in motion. For this reason, I like to use the word *harmony* instead of *balance*, because it more accurately describes what is possible. Stepping forward into the real you means intentionally operating in your unique strengths and passions and deliberately structuring your schedule to live more consistently in those areas.

Stepping Forward

- Go back to the section about awareness and answer the questions posed.
- What experiences have you had that significantly shaped who you are today?
- How might these experiences tie in to what you have to offer others to help them grow and step forward too?
- Journal your discoveries.

Endnotes

134 Laurie Beth Jones, *Jesus Life Coach: Learn from the Best* (Nashville, TN: Thomas Nelson, 2005), 298.

135 Laurie Beth Jones, *The Four Elements of Success: A Simple Personality Profile that Will Transform Your Team* (Nashville, TN: Thomas Nelson, 2005).

136 To find out more about the PEP™ and to receive your own personality report, visit my website: www.lisavanderkwaak.com/PEP.

137 Marcus Buckingham, *Find Your Strongest Life: What the Happiest and Most Successful Women Do Differently* (Nashville, TN: Thomas Nelson, 2009), 8.

138 Ibid., 138.

chapter twenty

Your Uniqueness Completes the Potential of Others

If only we could be as we truly are. This world would be changed in an instant.[139]

—Laurie Beth Jones

As a young entrepreneur, Ty Bennett had an opportunity to meet best-selling author Stephen Covey, and he was impacted by something Covey shared during a private conversation. Covey said, "The funny thing about life is that most people think that life is about achievement—about 'What can I get? How can I grow? What can I be rewarded for?' And the truth is, life is really about contribution. It's about helping people. It's about serving people."[140]

Here is a great nugget of wisdom: life is about contribution. Your uniqueness is your contribution to the world around you, and by living your uniqueness you express love towards God and others. The single most important goal of humans is this: *"'You must love the Lord your God with all your heart, all your soul, all your strength, and all your mind.' And, 'Love your neighbor as yourself'"* (Luke 10:27). The writer of the book of Romans says that as you offer your bodies to God as a living sacrifice, you are actually demonstrating an act of worship, or love, towards Him (Romans 12:1). Later in that same chapter, the writer elaborates on this, pointing out that each person has different gifts and we need to see them as being given to us for the purpose of serving others (Romans 12:6–8).

The well-known scientist Sir Isaac Newton developed several laws of physics that have since formed the foundation for countless other inventions and theories. I want to draw attention to one of his laws in particular, the Third Law of Motion, which states that for every action there is an equal and opposite reaction. For the sake of illustration, consider a fish. As the fish flaps its fins, the water exerts a force that is equal in strength but opposite in direction. This allows the fish to swim through the water. If there were not an equal and opposite force of action, the fish would remain stuck, its push only serving to stir up the water.

What does this have to do with loving people? Well, this law also means that for every interaction in nature, there is a pair of forces acting in mutually beneficial manner. The forces are equal in value and different in how they "push" on the environment.

Ephesians 4:16 says that God *"makes the whole body fit together perfectly. As each part does its own special work, it helps the other parts grow, so that the whole body is healthy and growing and full of love"* (emphasis added).

What this passage tells us is that as you do your own special work by offering your strengths and gifts in an area of life, you help other people to grow and mature. Just like applying its force in one direction allows the fish to swim, intentionally operating in your areas of strength will cause other people to act in their strengths as well. This is a powerful principle which highlights how essential it is for you to keep offering your unique self to the world around you.

Living true to who you are is an expression of love for God, yourself, and others. By living in this way, you acknowledge that what you have been given is to be invested in the lives of the people around you. As you become freer to live the real you more consistently, you will find that your life inspires and empowers others to be fully released into their divine purpose. As they, in turn, operate in their uniqueness, you will be empowered to live more fully. The more you allow yourself to flow in your unique strengths and gifts, the more you will find yourself walking in your calling and inspiring others to do the same.

Lance Wallnau confirmed this concept when I heard him say that every time you operate in your gifts, you "complete the potential of other people."[141] As you embrace the truth of your true identity and step forward to make your unique contribution to the world, keep in mind that by doing so you become a catalyst for others to step forward and more fully live out their potential. This is an amazing honour you have been given.

Freedom to Live Your Uniqueness

Becoming fully alive requires a process of transformation and freedom to occur in your heart and mind. This process is activated the moment you become born again and find yourself wanting to live like Jesus did. True freedom is a good indicator of the presence of the Spirit in your life. I realize that freedom can mean different things to different people, though, so I want to outline what freedom means from a biblical perspective.

Many years ago, while studying at Regent College in Vancouver, British Columbia, I took a course from a visiting professor named Howard Hendricks. That course was one of my favourites, mainly because Hendricks was a creative teacher and taught the importance of living creatively as a Christian. His book *Color Outside the Lines* is about developing creative leaders, and interwoven throughout is the fact that part of God's plan for your life is to bring you into a place of complete freedom in Christ.

Jesus Himself said that knowing the truth makes you free. The very presence of the Holy Spirit in your life will be seen by the degree that you walk in freedom. Although my highest core value is freedom, I'm not suggesting that it become yours. However, it's a strong and vital motivator to keep you moving forward when you face an obstacle. The truth is that freedom is a value of Kingdom living.

Inspired by Hendricks's writings, here are four areas to consider as you purpose to walk in freedom daily.

1. Acceptance of responsibility. Freedom means that you have a choice in how you act. However, it doesn't mean that you're free to escape the consequences of your actions. As an illustration, consider the law of gravity. You may not believe in or understand the law, but that will not change the fact that if you jump from a high cliff you will feel the pain of ignoring it. Hendricks says that "our assignment is to learn the benefits, to get on the good side of the 'law,' of the way the world operates."[142] By doing so, you can enjoy freedom "without needing to blame something or someone else for the consequences."[143] In doing so, you exercise freedom in choosing to do the right thing, although you can only experience freedom to the degree that you take personal responsibility.

2. Living the real you. Throughout this book, I have emphasized the fact that you have been uniquely designed. Hendricks says that "one of the most elusive assignments is to get people to be themselves. Invariably, they want to become like someone else, because they compare themselves with others rather than developing their own uniqueness."[144] The sooner you accept the truth about how God sees you, the sooner you will discover the freedom to live more authentically. The more secure you become in your identity and express more fully your uniqueness, the more of an impact you will have on the world around you. A further benefit of knowing and loving yourself is that you will gain increased understanding and insight into other people's uniqueness and needs.

3. Embracing reality. When you're walking in freedom, you are open to adventure, learning, and making further discoveries, including the freedom to fail. Hendricks says, "No one is a failure unless we fail to learn from our lack of success."[145] He suggests adopting this motto: "Nothing to prove, nothing to lose."

Hendricks adds that "people need to be preserved and protected from the disapproval of others," as that can kill them. Therefore, freedom also means being willing to affirm others in their worth and encouraging them to go back and redo that which they've missed or failed to complete. This will help them learn to view mistakes as learning opportunities and not to fear failure. This also encourages them to embrace the process of transformation and not adopt an "all or nothing" attitude of perfection.

Freedom involves being willing to embrace mistakes and trials as opportunities to grow and learn as you engage the Spirit's power to move you forward. The psalmist put it like this: *"I've learned that there is nothing perfect in this imperfect world except your words, for they bring such fantastic freedom into my life!"* (Psalm 119:96, TPT).

Embracing the truth of God's Word walks you down the path to freedom. When Jesus came on the scene on the earth, He was the full expression of Father God. He was the Word of God fully expressed in human form. He was and is the Truth. The Greek word for "truth" actually means "reality." Embracing the reality of Christ in your life expands your capacity to walk in freedom daily.

4. Having direction and control. Hendricks suggests, "Many Christians are stained and scarred because two powerful agents—scripture and the Holy Spirit—have been missing (or unbalanced) in their lives and work."[146] Both Scripture and the Holy Spirit are there to provide you with loving guidance for your life. If you have too much direction and control, you'll be hindered from becoming all that you are capable of becoming. But too little direction results in dangerous eruptions of unresolved issues of the heart. Freedom doesn't mean doing what you want, wherever you want; it means having access to creative imagination, innovative thinking, and divine wisdom to know the right thing to do and have the power to do it.

Living in complete freedom simply means that you're free on the inside, empowered to make a choice; you aren't leaning on others to make that choice for you. And secondly, having freedom means that you're free to choose the right way instead of the popular way. You are no longer enslaved to patterns of behaviour that leave you feeling helpless and hopeless.

The fruit of being spiritually free shows up in relationships. Your ability to receive and give love wholeheartedly in any area of your life exists in direct proportion to the degree that you're able to experience freedom in the deeper levels of your heart. Gaining freedom and wholeness is an essential pursuit if you are to step forward, live the real you, and fulfill your unique calling. Without this, you will continue to live someone else's life.

Remember, it was for our freedom that Christ died. Years before, the psalmist foretold it: *"But the Lord has paid for the freedom of his servants, and he will freely pardon those who love him. He will declare them free and innocent when they turn to hide themselves in him"* (Psalm 32:22, TPT, emphasis added).

Have you turned to hide yourself in Christ? If so, He has declared you free. Now step forward today with confidence, rooted in the truth, and fully experience the power of living the real you.

Stepping Forward

- If you were to adopt the motto "Nothing to prove, nothing to lose," what difference would it make in your everyday choices?
- How has your view changed about what it means to walk in freedom?
- In what areas of your life do you need to include one or both of these powerful agents: Scripture and the Holy Spirit?
- Journal your discoveries.

Endnotes

139 Jones, *Jesus Life Coach*, 298.

140 Heard during a live webinar.

141

142 Hendricks, *Color Outside the Lines*, 73.

143 Ibid.

144 Ibid.

145 Ibid.

146 Ibid., 74.

chapter twenty-one

Unique Contributions

Doing something for others helps us see the power we have to effect change. It can help put life in perspective.[147]

—Valorie Burton

In ancient Israel, women were seen as less important than men and treated as second-class citizens. Sadly, this practice still happen in many cultures around the world today. However, there is a growing awareness worldwide of the importance of men and women working alongside each other in making the world a better place. I personally believe that when men and women learn to love, honour, and value each other as equal partners in life and learn to function in their unique gifts, the image of God will be more accurately reflected on the earth. I believe this was God's original intent. Whether you're male or female isn't important in God's eyes; both are important and have been designed to make a difference on the earth. The world needs the contributions of both working together in unity of heart and mind to fulfill the greater purpose and allow God's glory to fill the earth.

This concept is still a struggle for many people to accept. For the purposes of this book, I want to examine how the unique contribution of one woman in biblical history caught God's attention and the effect it had on others. The woman's name is Rahab, and she is first introduced in the second chapter of the book of Joshua as a prostitute. First of all, it wasn't common practice for women to be named in ancient Hebrew documents, especially if the woman was considered to be unrighteous. So the fact that Rahab is included by name and that her story is told suggests that her past experiences didn't disqualify her from being used of God. I believe it was her *response* that caught God's attention.

As the story is told, two Israelite men were sent to spy out the city of Jericho and they stayed the night at her place. Have you ever wondered why they chose to stay there? Most likely it was because of the vantage point of her house, which was built on the wall that surrounded Jericho. The spies asked if they could hide in her home for the night, and she responded in kindness. This one act of hospitality opened a door to a whole new way of living for her and her family. She probably had no idea that this would happen; she simply made a decision that she would help the spies, at great risk to herself and her family. The Israelite spies could have judged her, afraid that her past experiences and current lifestyle would corrupt their community if they allowed her and her family to come with them. Instead they saw beyond that and into her heart, and they chose to reward her for her kindness. As a result, Rahab and her family were spared the disaster that came upon Jericho.

Sometime after that, Rahab accepted another type of invitation, which was to marry an Israelite man named Salmon. You will discover at Rahab's name is listed in the genealogy in Matthew 1:1–11, showing that through her marriage to Salmon and the eventual birth of her son Boaz, she became part of the lineage of Jesus Christ. Considering that Jewish protocol was not to list the names of the women in the genealogies, I think God wanted us to know that it doesn't matter where you come from and what has happened in your past, it is the posture of your heart and response to His invitations that are most important. Men and women are of equal value in the kingdom of heaven.

In order to successfully live out your unique purpose on the earth, you have to choose to accept the invitation to spiritually connect to Him as your source of life and trust Him step by step. It's really not about us, but about what He has already done and can do through us if our hearts are willing.

Rahab dared to believe that God could take a mess and turn it into a life-changing message. She let go of her past to pursue God's plan. She embraced the process of transformation and became instrumental in bringing about God's plan of redemption, which continues to impact generations even today.

As you learn to embrace the real you and discover the unique blend of experiences, personality, skills, passions, and strengths that you've been given, you will begin investing generously into the lives of others. As you give out of what you have been given, your life will become richer and more fulfilled. Your confidence and passion will increase and your personal capacity will grow, allowing you to accomplish things you previously thought were beyond your reach. Most importantly, you will also experience a stretching of your heart's capacity to live more fully connected, more fully committed, to God through every interaction you have with others.

There is a famous story in Matthew 25:1–30 about a king who gave three of his servants a portion of money to invest for him while he was away. When he returns, he discovers that two of the servants did what he asked and doubled their investment. The third servant did nothing with the amount he was given except bury it in the ground, thus his investment did not increase beyond its original size. The story is meant to illustrate the importance of being faithful to invest whatever you have been given, whether it's your time, talent, material wealth, or other personal asset. No gift is too insignificant. Your responsibility is to use it, invest it in the lives of others, and trust God for the outcome.

In the latter part of the story, the king rewards the two servants for their faithfulness by giving them even more money, and in modern terms he gave them a job promotion. The lesson of the story is summarized in this verse: *"To those who use well what they are given, even more will be given, and they will have an abundance"* (Matthew 25:29). If you want to be able to move to the next level in your life, start by functioning in the gifts you have been given and contribute to other people's lives by offering to give what only you can give—your uniqueness.

The writings of the apostle Peter serve to remind us that God has given each of us gifts and that we are to manage them well so that God's generosity can flow through us to others (1 Peter 4:10). Your life has meaning, and your personality and gifts are connected to your unique purpose.

The difficult experiences of life can try to rob you of this truth. In the midst of trial and tribulation, it's often hard to see purpose and have hope. Yet it is through these experiences that God wants to forge your character and create in you a strong sense of security and intimate connection with him. Knowing God as your source of life and love will increase your level of fulfillment. Embracing His truth and receiving Him as your source of love on a daily basis will expand your capacity to give love and walk in freedom and wholeness.

You may be like so many people and find yourself working at a job you hate, dissatisfied with life. You may have settled for less because the money was good or predictable. You may be in a place where your presence in someone's life brings them hope and inspiration. Whatever the situation, ask God what His purpose is for you and how His generosity can be more fully expressed through you as you offer your unique contributions to those around you.

In her book *Jesus, Career Counselor*, Laurie Beth Jones encourages you to, "Do not live beneath your own dreams nor God's dreams for you."[148] Don't settle for simply a comfortable life when you are meant to experience a fulfilling life full of adventure and intimacy.

I once heard Kent M. Keith speak about a booklet he wrote in 1968, when he was nineteen years old. These writings contained what he called the Paradoxical Commandments. It wasn't until thirty years later that he realized what a huge impact his book had had on major organizations and leaders around the world. Keith attended a Rotary meeting one day and heard a friend of his give a speech. Mother Teresa had passed away just weeks before, so his friend gave a tribute to her. In his tribute, he quoted a poem called "Anyway" which he said she had written. As Keith listened, he realized that the poem had actually been taken from his own book and was part of his Paradoxical Commandments! Afterwards, he went up to the speaker and asked where he had gotten the information.

"It was from a book about Mother Teresa," the speaker said. "It is a great poem."

"Yes," Keith replied. "I wrote that thirty years ago."

Later, Keith discovered that the poem had been posted on Mother Teresa's wall because she had read it in his book. Here is the version of the poem that was posted on her wall:

ANYWAY
People are unreasonable, illogical, and self-centered,
LOVE THEM ANYWAY
If you do well, people will accuse you of selfish, ulterior motives,
DO GOOD ANYWAY
If you are successful, you win false friends and true enemies,
SUCCEED ANYWAY
The good you do will be forgotten tomorrow,
DO GOOD ANYWAY
Honesty and frankness make you vulnerable,
BE HONEST AND FRANK ANYWAY
What you spent years building may be destroyed overnight,
BUILD ANYWAY
People really need help but may attack you if you help them,
HELP PEOPLE ANYWAY
Give the world the best you have and you'll get kicked in the teeth,
GIVE THE WORLD THE BEST YOU'VE GOT ANYWAY.

Christian singer Martina McBride has also written a song by the same name, which may have been inspired by this same poem. You never know what impact you'll have until you step forward and start living the real you!

Your greatest asset is Christ in you. As Christ becomes more and more at home in your heart, you will experience increased levels of wholeness. You'll discover the real you who is hidden in Christ and be empowered to walk in true freedom. Living the real you is one of the most powerful gifts you can offer to others. As Marcus Buckingham has said, "Find a new way to contribute a strength this week, and quite soon you will see the world realign itself to accelerate and increase this contribution."[149]

Have you ever heard someone practicing a piece of music and occasionally play what seemed like a wrong note? Well, in music there are no wrong notes, just misplaced ones. Are you living true to your authentic self or are you trying to live up to other people's expectations?

Laurie Beth Jones said, "If only we could be as we truly are. This world would be changed in an instant."[150]

I want to invite you to begin today by cultivating relationships that engage the heart and embracing the process of transformation so that you can become whole and free to express who you were created to be. You have also been given a fresh opportunity to align your heart to God's and faithfully invest your uniqueness in making a difference in the lives of others. To truly love God, and love your neighbour as yourself, you must accept that you have been wired for connection and embrace life fully with every action you take.

What are you waiting for? Life is way too short. Make a decision today and every day to let the real you step forward now!

Stepping Forward

- In what areas of your life can you start offering your uniqueness to add value to people around you?
- Who can you call upon to keep you accountable in stepping forward no matter what obstacles you face?
- What is the biggest insight you've taken away from reading this book?
- Share your insights with a friend or mentor and start implementing what you have learned.
- Journal your discoveries.

Endnotes

147 Burton, *Where Will You Go from Here?* 216.

148 Laurie Beth Jones, *Jesus, Career Counselor* (New York, NY: Howard Books, 2010), 40.

149 Buckingham, *Find Your Strongest Life*, 139.

150 Jones, *Jesus, Life Coach*, 298.

Conclusion

It has been my delight to journey with you through these pages to discover the five keys to walking in wholeness and freedom. As you carefully consider each key and reflect on how it applies to your life, I encourage you to set a goal to take the steps necessary to live according to your unique design every day.

1. Engage in heart-centred relationships with God, yourself, and others. Discover your true identity in Christ and live according to His thoughts towards you.
2. Embrace the process of transformation and don't let your heart get cluttered with unresolved issues. Every day do a soul cleanse!
3. Align your actions to the Truth. Seek to know the Truth and actively receive His love daily to experience true freedom.
4. Live the real you. Don't settle for anything less than having a heart that is whole and free to express your true self and to experience the fullness of God in every aspect of life.
5. Offer your unique gifts to be faithful with what you have been given, and in so doing you will enrich the lives of others. Walk fully in your purpose and know that by living true to the real you, you empower others to walk in their uniqueness too!

Letting the Real You Step Forward Now is ultimately about learning how to experience wholeness and freedom so that you can step forward to fulfill your unique calling on the earth. Remember, change is an essential part of experiencing freedom. No matter what you are facing, make a commitment to embrace transformation, submit to the work of the Holy Spirit within you, and let Him empower you to step forward every day.

A powerful catalyst to propelling you forward is making a decision to live life fully, including facing trials with an expectation of growth. Equally powerful is choosing to live more consistently in your areas of greatest strengths. As you do, your purpose will become clearer and decisions more streamlined. If you're still in a place of identifying your strengths, I encourage you to invest whatever time is needed to bring you clarity in this area. It will bring you tremendous joy and freedom to live the life you long for. There are various tools and programs on my website designed to do just that.[151]

I invite you to send an email to let me know what was the most valuable insight you received from this book and how you are letting the real you step forward. It will be such a joy to hear from you.

May you be strengthened daily as you engage your heart, embrace your process, and express your unique self in every facet of life!

Keep letting the real you step forward... every day.

Endnotes

151 See www.lisavanderkwaak.com.

Coming Soon

Pursue Fullness: Escape the Traps of Perfection, Performance & Passivity
By Lisa Vanderkwaak

Have you ever wondered if life as you know it is less than what God intended for you? Having a relationship with Jesus Christ gives you access to a life that's nothing less than what Jesus demonstrated during His time on the earth.

In fact, you and I were designed to experience a greater demonstration of God's power and presence than what even Jesus modelled. The miraculous works He performed were only a sampling of what you and I are created to walk in.

Why then do we settle for less than what's possible? Instead of walking in the Spirit without measure, as Jesus did, we settle for a trickle of power and struggle to maintain peace in our daily lives.

Why do most Christians not experience the overcoming power and overflowing joy that Jesus came to bring? I believe it has to do with our focus. For so long we have been told to pursue perfection as if it is something to be attained. In fact, it isn't.

In *Pursue Fullness*, Lisa Vanderkwaak will introduce you to a way of living that looks different, feels different, and produces different results than what you thought was possible. It's not based on performance or getting it right. Instead it's based on embracing your true identity, who you really are, and sharing in the divine nature of God.

Pursuing a lifestyle of fullness means engaging the truth wholeheartedly, believing that the way Jesus lived and operated on the earth is how you have been designed to live. It means accessing the resources of God to do more with what you have been given, and live with irresistible love, joy, and anointing. This will involve living outside the box that others may try to put you in.

The biblical truths you discover in this book will forever change the way you do life. They will ignite your passion and disrupt the status quo. Are you ready to see the realities of heaven manifested on the earth as you learn how to pursue fullness and escape the traps of performance, perfectionism, and passivity?